50 YEARS (
SOUTH MID
1921 – 1970

Written by David Flitton
Published by Paul Lacey

50 YEARS OF
SOUTH MIDLAND
1921 – 1970

**Written by David Flitton, designed and published by Paul Lacey,
17 Sparrow Close, Woosehill, Wokingham, Berkshire, RG41 3HT**

Acknowledgements

Any research of this nature relies on the contributions of many people, no matter how small. The author and publisher wish to express their gratitude to these individuals and groups for help with information or the use of photographs, with the usual apology for anyone overlooked:-

Pat Stokes (nee Beesley), Win Heath (nee Lynch), Robert Benstead, Arthur Langridge, Reg Hibbert, Arthur Waldron and Tom Pruett., from the ranks of SM and their families, together with enthusiasts Chris Taylor (HCVS), Brian Coney Derek Bradfield (PSVC), Dave Brubier (PHRG), John Bennett (OS), Keith Healey, Bob Kell, Roger James, and Ron Maybury.

On the photographic front we are indebted to the Omnibus Society Library, and in particular the extensive work of R H G Simpson and Martin Shaw. A number of other photographs are unmarked and cannot be acknowledged.

Dedication

The author would like to dedicate this work to his Mum and Dad

Contents

OTHER TITLES IN THIS SERIES

The Independent Bus & Coach Operators of the Newbury Area, 1919 – 1932 <u>Now out of print</u>
A review of the early operators in the area prior to the formation of Newbury & District, published 1985,
164 pages A5, card covers, ring bound, 42 illustrations and area map. Includes the Country Carriers.

A History of Newbury & District Motor Services Ltd., 1932 – 1952
<u>Now out of print</u>
The intricate story of the origins and development of this most interesting operator, published 1987, 309 pages A5, laminated covers, ring bound, 130 half-tones, route maps, full fleet list, line drawings.

A History of the Penn Bus Co. Ltd., 1920 –1935   **£2.50**
An intimate portrait of this dynamic High Wycombe area independent, published 1990, 48 pages A5, card covers, folded, 26 half-tones, route map, full fleet list, written with the assistance of the Sugg family.

Thames Valley – The British Years, 1915 –1920   **£2.95**
The pre-history of Thames Valley, covering the early triumphs and tribulations of local operations, published 1990, 52 pages A5, card covers, folded, 30 half-tones, route map, full fleet list, line drawings.

A History of the Thames Valley Traction Co. Ltd., 1920 –1930   £15.00
The detailed history of this vibrant period, including the 207 other operators sharing the roads with TV, published 1995, 144 pages A4, perfect bound, 144 half-tones, route map, full fleet list, line drawings.

Thackray's Way – A Family in Road Transport   **£10.00**
*An in-depth study of this enterprising family, written with assistance from their descendants, published 2001, 136 pages A5, perfect bound, 62 half-tones, plans of premises, route maps, full fleet list. **This is essential ''Thames Valley' reading.***

A History of the Thames Valley Traction Co. Ltd., 1931 – 1945   £25.00
The detailed account of the busy 1930's with consolidation through takeovers, then into the dark days of the Second World War, published 2003, 208 pages A4, perfect bound, nearly 300 half-tones, full fleet list, service vehicles and garaging details.

Written by Paul Lacey - all titles in print are available direct from the publisher, post free, or through good book suppliers.

Introduction

From an early age I took a keen interest in public transport, in some ways surprising, as the only contacts I had in this field were my father and mother, and their foray was relatively brief. My father, originally from Cambridge, had decided to get demobbed in this area after World War Two, as when he had joined the Royal Air Force in early 1938, amongst many short postings in this country prior to spending most of the war in North Africa and the Middle East, he spent time at Harwell, between Newbury and Oxford, which served as an operational base before and during the war. Out of some ten geographical locations in both England and Scotland he was sent to, a whistle stop tour, he fell in love with Berkshire and the surrounding area, and promised himself this is where he would settle down if he made it through the hostilities.

For no particular reason he ended up working as a driver for the Thames Valley Traction Co. Ltd. at the Reading depot after the war, where he met my mother who also worked for TV, as she spent the mid to late war years as a conductress based at the Newbury outstation servicing only the Newbury-Reading route. They managed to carry out their courting, rather curiously I suppose, mainly through meetings on layovers when they met at Reading, however not too much time passed before they were married, my mother later leaving TV to give birth to me, and as she lived in Newbury my father joined Newbury & District Motor Services Ltd. Later when I was able to understand, my mother would recall quite graphically some of the journeys she made, usually relating to weather problems, as the buses at Newbury were open staircase, but the most extraordinary had to be the two or three times she literally walked all the way from Reading to Newbury in front of the bus with a torch for some 17 miles, due to a combination of blackout precautions and what was known then as 'pea-soupers', very thick fog or 'smog' as it was sometimes called.

My father claimed a total lack of interest in buses and coaches, and yet if approached when he was in a good mood the information would start flowing, recalling much about the Associated Motorway relief hiring's he would carry out. These could see him in the summer season away for several days at a time, and although this might only mean he was in a semi circle of Bournemouth, Bristol, Cheltenham, Birmingham, Northampton, Oxford down to Newbury with several London trips for AM, he would explain how difficult it was sometimes to get that hiring back to Newbury itself, many times finding he would be about turned and start heading away from base when he may only be 25 miles from Newbury though often much further afield than that.

He would also mention numerous companies he had come across, which I would list, and to be honest even at that early age I became sceptical as to if all the names really existed as companies, as travelling to other parts of the country rarely happened in the early fifties so I had no way of proving or otherwise their existence. As I got older it has to be said the list was authenticated one by one, if not by literally seeing the vehicles, or I would read of the names in periodicals of the times or in advertisements and, however obscure the name, I found eventually it did exist - so much for someone uninterested! He confessed he enjoyed his time at N & D, and I think this is because of the particular duties he was tasked with, which seemed to be overwhelmingly coaching. When Newbury & District was taken over by Thames Valley, his stay with them was short, about a year I think and he never ever was involved in the industry again. My mother did however return to work for Thames Valley, serving in the Newbury enquiry office in the early to mid sixties when I was a teenager.

So this is the only reason I can think an interest in this industry occurred, although it has to be said it virtually died on the forming of the National Bus Company. It had been on my mind for some years to compile a history of Newbury & District, however time never seemed to be available, and Paul Lacey's publication did indeed do justice to that fine company, though I only knew it had been published many years after the release date. Nostalgia then crept back, so I decided I would like to compile a history of the South Midland Company, which was also close to my heart.

Believe me, I don't recommend choosing a business that has been out of existence for many decades, but in essence ceased in 1950 in the historical sense of an independent company. It has been mind blowing, and I just hope the result will be regarded as worthwhile by readers. The one driving force has been Paul Lacey, who when I approached him in the beginning to enquire if he would be prepared to allow photos from his collection to be included, informed me immediately ' If its not a worthy history you will not get any prints from me'. But seriously, Paul is a great guy to have on your case, and I owe him great debt of gratitude for his time, and knowledge of where to obtain information from and duly agreeing to publish the result. Many thanks Paul.

David Flitton, Hungerford, July 2004

Chapter One One Man's Vision

In the years immediately following the First World War, as indeed it has to be said of following the unfortunate Second World War some twenty seven years later, people became battle weary. They had endured an environment of doom and gloom for four years, thousands of individuals had perished on the battlefield and during this time survival became the name of the game, so thoughts of anything other than the depressing circumstances most found themselves under were just that, thoughts. Hopes of idyllic days in the countryside or by the coast lay in the future, the war seemingly to last a lifetime, and such dreams provided the only crumbs of comfort to many during this period.

However, as a new dawn arose in 1918, individuals became impatient to explore the new freedom peacetime brought. They wanted away from the claustrophobic urban areas in which many of them lived, wanted to smell fresh air of the countryside, taste sea-water as they swam or just play on the beaches. In many instances, those individuals had never experienced these things, the highlight of the week, if they were lucky, a trip on a Sunday to the local park. Wartime restrictions had, by necessity, been severe and nowhere more so than in the area of free movement. Therefore it is not at all difficult given this scenario, that any individual with an ounce of entrepreneurial flair would have sensed this need for travel arising, and have taken steps to supply the means by which this yearning could be fulfilled.

Having a good idea is one thing, but being able to put that idea into practice is another, and as with any business plan, the obvious first requirement is the capital required. It would be fair to say that using the desciption business plan to many starting up a business just after the First World War, those soldiers who had returned home at last now receiving their gratuities and almost instantly starting some sort of venture, the term meant nothing. In the main anyone mentioning such a prerequisite would have been looked at in a rather blank fashion. Such probably were the circumstances, as already outlined, that one William Beesley found himself under, spotting a niche market for the charabanc.

Not for William the obvious route of many ex servicemen, using their hard won cash to purchase an ex War Department lorry, often extremely basic, convert it to carry a few passengers, then become what today would be described (certainly in the road haulage market) as an owner driver, more often than not though, referred to in this era and in this industry as a 'pirate'. Individuals who had now achieved an ability to drive, through enlistment in the Army, a very basic understanding in many instances, viewed the idea of carrying people to wherever, as a way of making a 'quick buck '. However very necessary in this era was a knowledge of the internal combustion engine, an obvious essential element for survival, not least to gain the upper hand against the competition that was rife.

Mechanics existed of course, but using the services of such individuals who were also out to make a living, and a very good one if circumstances allowed, was certain to take an unhealthy percentage of turnover. Eventually disheartened by the results of their endeavours, large numbers decided to either call it a day, or more often than not, had that decision taken away from them by being declared bankrupt. Yes there were those who did survive for longer periods, but they were in the minority, and generally sold out to a new breed of larger operators that emerged in the mid to late 'twenties, as they made their presence felt.

William Frank Beesley, to give him his full name, had been trained in engine mechanics in the Army. Indeed, his Daughter recalled being told by her Father how he had tried to enlist, as did many of his fellow countrymen at that time when under age, to fight for King and Country, but did not succeed, due to what she described as his obvious youthful looks at the time in question. However, at the first legal opportunity in 1916 immediately signed up. On exiting the forces, William Beesley sat examinations for entry into the Civil Service which he passed, possibly with distinction, for not only did he then enter the Forestry Commission department, but appears to have had the ear of a Mr William Ling Taylor. His significance will become apparent, and whom it appears held fairly high office, so it is logical to assume, William was what today would be described as a ' fast track ' manager to have had the ear of such exalted company.

This then would have been the background under which WFB, having perceived of the potential of travel all around him decided on his plan, which as he saw it, took into consideration the mistakes being made by his fellow countrymen in the transportation market. It is not beyond the realms of possibility that the original intention might have been the haulage industry, given that a photograph exists of William with a Hallford lorry, which would indicate this direction of thought. Possibly it had been discussed to run both types of transport, given the railway strike of 1919, which lasted from the 26th September until the 6th October of that year, which to put it bluntly had paralysed the country.

The Hallford lorry as it arrived direct from the Army disposal sale.

William then, armed with the essential business plan information, plus a very obvious 'gut feeling ' about this new exciting industry taking root quite rapidly, would have approached his boss Mr Taylor. Although hard to determine the exact nature of their relationship, it would most certainly have been one of mutual respect, very unusual at this point in time, especially given Beesley would have only been twenty or twenty one years of age. Then again what it does tell us about Taylor, is that he was likely to have been a man ahead of his time, both in vision and ideas, and in all probability saw Beesley as a younger version of himself with the additon of raw youthful energy.

Adept in business matters, as no doubt William Taylor was, and with serious connections in the industrial and financial sectors, he would have taken advice on any business initiative, even one originating from his protégé. What that advice may have been one can only speculate, for my money Taylor would have submittcd it as his own idea to gauge unbiased opinion, and made a balanced judgement on what he heard. I am sure that will not all have been positive, as the railways still seen as the way forward. At this point after having made his decision, I believe it is probable William Beesley was instructed by Taylor to 'test the market'. It is purely speculation on my part, but I think it is possible this indeed took place using a converted ex War Department truck (the Hallford maybe?), albeit for a brief period only, possibly late 1920 or very early 1921, also to check if WFB was as good as the credentials he was waving.

Certainly on the 1st April 1921 the Oxford Times carried a small article which purported to advise of a large business scheme, under the auspices of the 'South Midland Touring and Transport Company'. With headquarters at Lloyds Bank Chambers Oxford, it was to be entirely staffed by Oxford ex-servicemen and would only operate up-to-date char-a-bancs. The fact that the article mentions that a few trips had already been operated does indicate a trial period, although the article goes on to say about the company's considerable experience of char-a-banc tours. Given the known facts and the previous statement in the article regarding limited operation, I think it is safe to conclude that South Midland and its owners were very much newcomers in the passenger-carrying field.

In the same issue of the Oxford Times, South Midland placed an advertisement essentially confirming the newspaper article contents, with the specific detail of the vehicle type 'Look out for the Grey Torpedo Coaches', by then a description suggesting a char-a-banc of Dennis manufacture. This same statement confirmed William Beesley's shrewd thinking, to put the company immediately ahead of much of the competition, with a vehicle of very good repute. To choose such a vehicle would indeed prove to be fortuitous, for what lay ahead in the coming months would surprise many, not least everyone involved in the new venture.

One of the original fleet of Dennis charas shown on a trip to Southsea.

Dennis Brothers of Guildford had already built up an enviable reputation for a reliable chassis, prior to its production being switched to meet the war effort. Following the cessation of hostilities, the company quickly began to produce large numbers of its standard design of 'torpedo' charabancs, these being mounted on a 2.5 ton chassis and fitted with the efficient and reliable 40hp engine built by its White & Poppe subsidiary at its Coventry factory in the Midlands. The vehicles were regarded by the industry as the Rolls Royce of chara's, the interior specification featuring seats for thirty passengers which were upholstered by the then famous furnishers of Waring & Gillow. The majority of production tended to be finished in a very light grey colour, often described as 'silver' by many, but equally described as grey, the latter description chosen by the South Midland company, and used throughout its advertising literature.

An advertisement on the 13th May 1921 in the Oxford Times, that newspaper being used as a regular publicity medium for some time to promote the company's activities, gave an indication of what Beesley had probably been thinking, and had no doubt formed the basis of the proposal he had put to Mr Taylor. This not only made the idea different at that point in time from others running char-a-bancs certainly in the Oxford area, but an attractive proposition to consider, with the financial backing ultimately being forthcoming. After listings of Whitsuntide excursions to the Malvern's, Berkshire Downs, Stratford-on-Avon and a circular tour of the Thames Valley, appeared an announcement of a regular Tuesday, Thursday and Saturday service to London (Marble Arch). Return fares only were offered at ten shillings, the departure time from Oxford 08.45 am arriving in London at 12 noon, the return journey leaving London at 06.45 pm to arrive back at Oxford at 10.00 pm.

The service travelled via Henley and Hounslow, and was scheduled to take three and a quarter hours, and as no indication is given of a refreshment break taken en route in the publicity material, I think it is safe to assume no such break was intended. This is therefore proof that despite what has been suggested by many of the transport 'experts', South Midland started their foray into express services in 1921, and not as generally stated in 1928 or later. According to the literature, passengers could join on route, though quite how this was to be achieved remains a mystery, given that it is unlikely agents had been appointed at this time.

It is perhaps inappropriate to recall a story of a 'man of Oxford', without first explaining the prominence of this city. It was, and still is, universally known as the 'City of Dreaming Spires', and has been a seat of learning for many hundreds of years, nearly nine hundred I believe. It became the head quarters of King Charles the First during the Civil War, and has always been an important city in many respects, not least its importance as a major crossroads of east to west and north to south traffic, which is extremely relevant to the South Midland story. At a distance from London of around sixty miles, in the past the travel link had been by water transport and stagecoach, both were later eclipsed by the coming of the railways, though the latter was now in a temporary state of turmoil in the early 'twenties. Population levels were, and would continue to be, a very important factor in the continuing success and expansion of the business. The numbers had swelled by some four hundred and fifty per cent from the early eighteen hundreds to the early nineteen hundreds, the level would again rise rapidly from a figure of some fifty odd thousand at the beginning of this story to well into a six figure number by the end of the period under review. The large student population has always accounted for an approximate figure of twenty per cent of Oxford's population, although this niche market has only likely to have been of importance to the South Midland since post World War Two.

Two chassis were ordered for the spring of 1921, the first materialising in April as FC 3902, followed in early May by FC 4010. A photo of the first South Midland charabanc was taken at Hyde Park in London, possibly on the inaugural run, with both William Beesley and his wife Ellen present. Indeed, it is possible William drove the vehicle himself on day one of the service at least, and is likely to have been on what later would be known as a 'layover', pending return to Oxford at 06.45 pm later in the day. In June of that year the London service became daily, Sundays excepted, and with an ever increasing excursion list, not to mention private hire work the company would have been diligently chasing, the reliability of the Dennis make would have become all too obvious. A minor adjustment in the timetable saw the London service departing fifteen minutes earlier at 08.30 am, to arrive in the capital a corresponding fifteen minutes earlier at 11.45 am. The return time unchanged, but it must have proved possible to do the return leg comfortably in three hours, as the arrival back at Oxford was now 09.45 pm, perhaps reflecting the lesser traffic during the evenings.

Ellen and William Beesley pose in the sunshine with Dennis FC 3902 at the London end of the pioneer South Midland route. Note that the vehicle is equipped with only an offside headlamp despite its largely rural route.

13

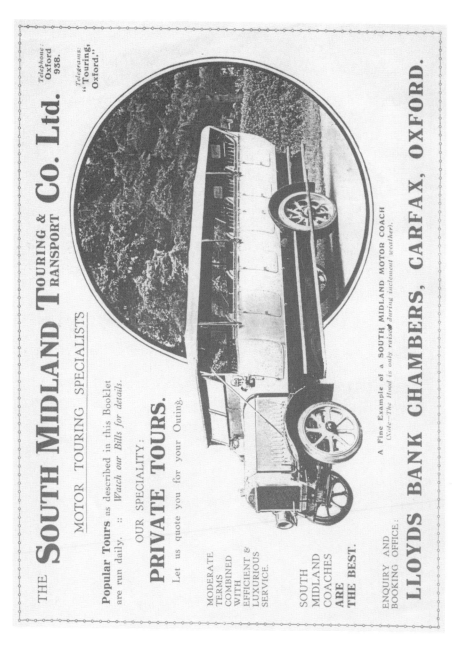

A page from the Tours Booklet, which included a Dennis charabanc, albeit sporting the Dennis trade plate P14A.

Chapter Two   Competition

The timetable for the Oxford-London express was beginning to take shape, for during June 1921 specific pick up points were publicised, those being at Dorchester (The Abbey), Benson (The Crown), Nettlebed (The Bull) and Henley (The Catherine Wheel Hotel), the last three mentioned also acting as the local booking agents, whilst that for Dorchester was the local Post Office. Departures from Oxford left the Clarendon Hotel in Cornmarket, as did all South Midland excursions. Again running times were adjusted, only to be expected given the infancy of the company and the lack of raw experience in house, and this saw fifteen minutes shaved off the journey to London, making it a three hour journey. The only adjustment to the return journey, which as previously mentioned was already down to three hours, was that it now left London at 06.30 pm. To broaden the range of fares, which it was hoped would encourage more traffic onto the route, a single fare of seven shillings and sixpence and a period return fare of fifteen shillings were introduced alongside the ten shillings day return.

Arguably as a result of increasing traffic congestion in London, or at least during the summer period, South Midland again reverted back to a scheduled time of three and a quarter hours for the journey time during the month of July 1921, and indeed this would remain the time allowed throughout the rest of the years operation in both directions, with the various departure and arrival times as follows:-

July   *Depart Oxford 08.30am arriving London 11.45am*
                  Depart London 06.30pm arriving Oxford 09.45pm

August   *Depart Oxford 08.30am arriving London 11.45am*
                  Depart London 06.15pm arriving Oxford 09.30pm

September   *Depart Oxford 08.30am arriving London 11.45am*
                  Depart London 06.00pm arriving Oxford 09.15pm

October   *Depart Oxford 08.30am arriving London 11.45am*
                  Depart London 06.00pm arriving Oxford 09.15pm

It is possible that with the daylight fading into the Autumn, travellers may have wished to commence their journey home at an earlier time, an early example of a public relations exercise maybe. Later during August, and the beginning of September, a Sunday service was provided, but the end of

October saw the cessation of the route for 1921. It is also indicative from the printed publicity available, that the period return probably ceased at the end of July in this year, perhaps on financial grounds. With the peaks and troughs of a business such as this, it may have necessitated on occasions, vehicles travelling empty to London to enable those passengers who had booked period returns to get back to Oxford, which was not a viable option. The other fares remained unchanged during the 1921 season.

Overcoats on and hats firmly in place, a chara party prepares to leave from the Iffley Road during June 1923. Note the young lady sitting on the outside of the driver, a common practice in those days! The fleetname is carried on the bonnet sides, and presumably also across the rear panel, in shaded gold lettering. Fleet numbers were introduced later on, but these Dennis charas had departed by that time.

Having mentioned earlier in the story Beesley's 'canny' choice of vehicle type, both reliable and well made, it soon proved an extremely wise option, as they would stand up to competition that was now about to erupt on the London route from a source that, I would guess even those involved in the South Midland venture, never expected to materialise! Towards the end of July 1921 City of Oxford Motor Services (from hereon referred to as COMS) decided to move in on this fledgling company, and again this information dispels the popular myth that COMS had never ever operated express services. More surprises of this nature will be revealed later on, though I digress. COMS obviously becoming very irritated that South Midland was succeeding in increasing its share of the excursion market, a preserve they considered theirs and theirs alone, and remember in Oxford at least, the authorities seemed totally biased towards COMS on all fronts. One need only look at the papers of the day to confirm the incestuous attitude that prevailed towards that company, as even the police ignored matters concerning COMS, such as for instance appointed drop and pick up points. Yet if an independent dared to carry out such a manoeuvre they would be booked, hence my point that COMS probably began to believe they were impregnable, and any business out of the City belonged to them!

An advertisement on the 22nd July 1921 in the Oxford Times gives the impression that detailed information had been conveyed elsewhere, and it might well have on placards locally, or equally logically on adverts placed on COMS own vehicles, which would have enabled it to try and steal a lead on the South Midland, even before that company had found its footings. The service announced by COMS covered the same route to London, left at the same time on the outward journey, though a fifteen minute break was allowed for at Henley. Although that increased the overall journey time by this amount (three and a quarter hours actual running time was given, the same as SM) it provided a much needed relief to passengers no doubt. The return leg left London fifteen minutes earlier in July than SM at 06.15 pm, again a break to be taken at Henley, arrival back at Oxford the same time as South Midland. During this month, no Sunday service operated, but perhaps somewhat more surprisingly, a return fare only was available (SM already had single fares), and it was at the same ten shillings as South Midland, as perhaps COMS hoped to trade on their good name for service. The Oxford departure point was the Carfax, whilst the London drop point was Marble Arch.

For August COMS lost no time in adopting a single fare of seven shillings and sixpence, again surprisingly matching South Midland, when one might have expected a fares war to develop. This the beginning of several mysteries surrounding SM in its history, which I will highlight throughout the story. Although I believe I have a plausible answer to them, confidentiality prevents me from explaining my theory regrettably, but I will give a clue for readers to make up their own minds much later on in the text. During mid August, for reasons unknown to the writer, COMS deviated from the route they were using, the express service now travelling from Oxford down the Thames Valley to Reading, where a fifteen minute break was taken, the journey then continuing via Staines, the return leg operating as normal with a break in Henley. Although one wonders if there were problems between the rival's drivers (see next paragraph), the more likely scenario is that it was thought a scenic trip with good long lasting views of the river might help encourage more business away from SM.

It is interesting to speculate what may have happened from time to time on this route, with similar timings and drivers being of a competitive nature. True in the case of South Midland, its drivers all ex military would have been well disciplined, with brothers Frank and Ted Surman the first and second drivers respectively of the company. But to be fair many of the COMS drivers would have also been from a similar background, and in my research, and though I would not call it exhaustive, I could find no record of incidents. So perhaps they all acted as Knights of the Road and were very polite to each other. If so it was not a scene generally mirrored in other parts of the country at this time, where competition was rife.

The 'river route' lasted all of one week, a nice idea but in reality I believe the drivers would have had difficulty in keeping to the scheduled times. These had not been altered, and to go via Staines, even in the 'twenties when traffic was sparse, was perhaps a deviation too far. However for the remainder of the operation of the service to London until it was halted by COMS at the end of September 1921, the outward route from Oxford still travelled to Reading and then Maidenhead along the main Bath Road, returning instead through Henley to Oxford. Fifteen minute breaks were still incorporated into the service at Reading and Henley, with the departure time from Marble Arch changed to 05.45 pm, which of course still ensured the time back to Oxford was the same as the South Midland service.

It is worth also noting, that by the summer of 1921, the advertised excursion lists of both SM and COMS, can be seen to be invoking a very competitive atmosphere, similar destinations listed, more often than not on the same days. Again, there is a mystery here, as the fares charged to the various destinations were identical in both cases. Perhaps it would be fairer to say that, because at this point in time SM were not that well versed in costing exercises, they tended to be conservative and rather than risk financial embarrassment priced the same as COMS - you pays your money etc. Although in a competitive environment, much as today in fact, it seems very strange a fares war did not start up. Broadly speaking, thus ended the 1921 season, which had been extremely competitive, and certainly South Midland's entry had been 'a baptism of fire' - though more was to come.

Chapter Three   Survival

1922 dawned and probably the South Midland staff were still a little 'shell shocked ' at the competitive response they had received from COMS the previous year. Over the winter period, business would appear to have only been generated from private hire work, no excursions being advertised, which was not unexpected given the charabanc was still fairly primitive. Only the very hardy would have travelled long or even medium distances during the winter season. However armed with blankets and hot water bottles, if required, there would have been no lack of customers wishing to hire a vehicle for local events, say within thirty miles or so, from football and rugby teams during the daytime. Evening hires for various public house dart teams were an example of a male preserve, but also equally local Women's Institutes and the like, very popular in these times, visiting associates in outlying villages, whilst some schools were now utilising this form of travel for local educational visits, so all in all the business would have ticked over, the drivers no doubt also required to make the occasional haulage journey using the lorry owned at that time. The opportunity would also have been taken to completely overhaul the charabancs ready for the spring season of nineteen twenty-two.

At the season's start, a significant event happened in the history of the company, in that it became a limited liability business. Particulars of the directors, under the Directors Act 1917, were forwarded to the authorities on the twenty ninth of March nineteen twenty two, the company being formally registered a few days later on the fourth of April. The directors were listed as follows: -

William Ling Taylor   *Robert Blakeman Eynan Trinder*
William Frank Beesley   *Clara Elizabeth Evelyne McCubbin*
Edith Muriel Theresa Taylor

Mrs McCubbin was William Taylor's widowed sister, and in fact lived with her brother and his wife Edith. Speaking to William Beesley's daughter whilst researching for this book, she was of the opinion, although without specific details, that her father at least (if not the rest of the directors) did not see eye to eye with Mr Trinder. In any case he had his directorship cut short, for by June of this year, he appears to have been removed from the list of directors, being replaced by Beesley's wife. The designated positions within the company held by the directors from June were as follows: -

Chairman	William Taylor
Managing Director	*William Beesley*
Company Secretary	*Ellen Beesley*

However despite the titles, William Beesley totally ran the business, and did so until the business was eventually sold on, although that was to be very much in the future. In May nineteen twenty-two, another new Dennis 2.5 ton vehicle was added to the fleet, again seating thirty persons and registered FC 4501. Also an elaborate booklet was produced, though surprisingly research has shown this not to be that unusual for the time, in which was listed forty eight excursions, though described as tours. Each tour was given a number one through to forty eight, and in over forty pages the excursions were described in amazing detail, a relevant location photograph accompanying each tour description.

The cover of the booklet depicted a Dennis, similar to those operated, however with a registration T 9512, obviously a template used as a standard cover for many operators of the day. Once opening the booklet, there was a foreword, which initially extols the virtues of travelling by motor coach, described as realising the 'Freedom of Beautiful Britain'. It further goes on to describe its employees as all ex servicemen etc., in reality a copy of the initial advertisement placed, then follows detail of the Dennis charabanc, although here again the template feature comes in, describing them as twenty eight seaters, this should have been changed to thirty seaters. The last part of the foreword is interesting, in that it states that 'taxation forms no small part of the cost of running, and the present taxes imposed upon the larger motor vehicles are exceedingly heavy', a noticeable political point if ever there was one. Next in the booklet came a detailed diagrammatic map illustrating each tour route, and a splendid map at that.

I think an assumption can safely be made, that due to the obvious difficulties in becoming established, nineteen twenty one would not have been a morale boosting year financially. Undeterred, excursions were considerably expanded for the 'twenty-two season, destinations advertised such as Bournemouth, Weston-Super-Mare, Ross-on-Wye, Epsom, Kempton, Ascot and Newbury races (a very popular outing), and at different times throughout the year, the majority of the tours listed in the published booklet were advertised in the local newspapers.

Opposite: *The front cover of the first edition of the fully illustrated and highly descriptive South Midland tours booklet.*

The London express service re-commenced in the latter part of March, departing daily from Oxford at 08.30 am. Returning from London at 06.30 pm, the journey time in both directions was three and a quarter hours. Perhaps surprised that South Midland were again pursuing this route, COMS entered the fray some three weeks later, offering a Tuesday, Thursday and Saturday service, from Oxford at 08.45 am returning from London at 05.45 pm. However two significant developments took place, the first, and perhaps an admission that SM had 'got it right ', the route now followed that taken by South Midland. No refreshment stops were made, so the journey time was the same. Customer choice came down to a preference of departure and arrival times. One can sense slightly at this point SM had the upper hand, for by the end of April it was advertising the London Zoo as an official stop, arriving at 11.45 am, then on to Marble Arch for 12.00 noon. The return journey was timetabled to leave the zoo at 06.15 pm, picking up at the Arch at 06.30 pm, giving day visitors six and a half hours at the zoo itself, or a combination of zoo and sightseeing.

Although there was a fifteen minute increase in travelling time, the convenience of the drop off point at such a major attraction, outweighed the few minutes of inconvenience for main destination passengers. Surprisingly COMS did not retaliate, but did increase its London service to include Monday, Wednesday and Friday, thereby offering a daily weekday service from May. For the rest of the year, the South Midland London express service remained unchanged, until it finished at the end of September, as indeed did COMS. The excursions advertised dipped over the June to August period, perhaps due to a greater success on not only the London service, but the trips to both Cheltenham and Stratford-on-Avon Although excursions with only return fares, they almost become mini express services, the former operating every Sunday, Tuesday, Thursday and Saturday the latter every Monday, Wednesday and Friday, both services pm departures and returns, requiring the allocation of one vehicle all week.

Although at first glance it would appear COMS might be winning the excursion business, with its much larger fleet providing more excursions, it was not to the detriment of South Midland business as a whole. The only variation on the competing COMS London service during the season, was for the departing time from Marble Arch during June, July and August to be set back to leave at 06.15 pm, visitors wishing to maximise the daylight hours. Six booking agents were appointed by South Midland in various areas of Oxford City, for the convenience of customers making bookings other than in central Oxford.

Chapter Four   Renaissance

Nineteen twenty three was perhaps a year for reflection, as noted at the statutory Annual General Meeting on the 1st August at Lloyds Bank Chambers in Oxford, which was attended by William Taylor, William Beesley and his wife Ellen. It would certainly have been recognised that, as in the first year of operation, the second year had also seen equally difficult trading conditions, recorded as ' due to the obvious difficulties in becoming established'. However not to be criticised for lack of optimism, it was also noted 'it was hoped the company would show a substantial increase in (business) the coming year', which indicated that even so far into this year things were still quite tough!

Whatever the business climate for South Midland, which looked a little bleak on the face of it, COMS was itself finding some difficulties, in spite of the expanding stage carriage work. It seems likely that talks took place between the two companies, probably in the early part of the year, regarding the London express service. Neither of the Companies re-started its service during the traditional Spring period, despite the Easter break usually providing much business to the Capital. When SM did commence at the start of May, it ran on a Monday, Wednesday and Friday, whilst COMS operated on Tuesday, Thursday and Saturday, SM rather surprisingly having agreed to accept some of the lean days of the week.

However, from June through to the end of September both concerns once again operated daily, with SM travelling via the London Zoo and COMS direct to Marble Arch (which was also part of a 'gentlemen's agreement' perhaps?). South Midland, one would assume due to public demand, changed the London departure time leaving the Zoo at 05.45pm and Marble Arch at 06.00pm. The excursion and private hire work continued to generate more passengers and therefore income, one hire worthy of note being the taking of one hundred school children from St Giles in Oxford to Middleton Park during July. However, whilst this increased business was most welcome and augured well for the Company's obvious enthusiasm, again an adverse trading result was reported when the accounts were presented at the AGM. The reason given was a fall in market value of the company's assets which had led to larger depreciation requiring to be written off than would normally have been expected. SM would therefore need to look carefully at its operating costs, together with making full use of its small fleet, including perhaps the addition of a smaller vehicle.

These circumstances intimate that a 'knock down' price was possibly paid for LK 8069 the secondhand Crossley sixteen-seater 'allweather' coach with central gangway and pneumatic tyres which joined the three Dennis's in October of this year. If nineteen twenty-three was a year of consolidation then nineteen twenty-four was the 'new beginning', the original vision of Beesley shared by his financial backer Taylor coming to fruition. This would be payback time for those tough early years, and would again highlight William's amazing ability to pre-judge events correctly, or then of course he may well have just been born under the right star!

The 16-seater Crossley provided a useful addition to the full-size charas.

For the older generations (of which I am a member) school geography lessons entailed learning that all the countries coloured pink on the world atlas, or more usual the world globe, 'belonged' to Great Britain. Political correctness not having arrived in this period, we were taught to be proud of this 'ownership' and it helped make Britain 'Great'. Despite movements by many of these countries towards independence, these were still early days in nineteen twenty four, and the British Empire (as the countries were collectively known) still covered twenty five per cent of the world's land mass. Quite a remarkable feat even today, if one stops and thinks about it long enough. However, with 'the sun never setting' on this vast area under British control, it had been decided by the government of the day to organise a huge exhibition called quite literally the British Empire Exhibition which would be held at the new sporting complex being built on the Wembley site in North London.

Throughout 1924 the original trio of Dennis charas carried the lion's share of South Midland traffic. The second of them (FC 4010) is seen that year with a full party from the Crown Inn.

The prime purpose was to stimulate trade, as unemployment was still a major problem in the country at large, whilst strengthening the bonds between the countries in the Empire, in fact a sort of party with representatives from every Empire country. This exhibition then, which was formally opened by King George V, would consist of the best that was achievable in exhibits to form a huge shop window to the world at large. It would be visited by millions of people from all around the world, and of course a good number from Oxfordshire, care of South Midland excursions.

For such a massive exercise it was imperative that official agents were appointed throughout the country to hand out information and be able to issue entry tickets for the exhibition itself. South Midland had made representations to be appointed Official District Agents, along with many others no doubt from within their area, again what I perceive as the 'right connections' saw this rather small company become appointed. The impact this had on the business was immense, such was the private hire advance bookings by various organisations that it was decided at an early stage in the year that operation of the London express to Marble Arch would have to be suspended!

As this service had been seasonal, it is probable that with the exhibition being the talking point of the year, with thousands wishing to visit, that few would have been inconvenienced by not being able to catch a coach to the central area of the City. However, it was soon recognised that not everyone would organise themselves into large enough groups to book a complete vehicle. Therefore when the opportunity arose at the beginning of June of this year, the summer holiday season in effect, a daily service to Wembley commenced which was to last until the end of October, such was the demand.

The fare charged was eight shillings and sixpence return or an all-inclusive ten shillings return incorporating the one shilling and sixpence admission, the latter alleviating the need to queue. Departure time from Oxford mirrored the London express when that was operating of 08.30am, return was however 07.00pm., the size of the venue and the time it would take to attempt to see all that was exhibited the most likely reason. COMS, who were a little 'miffed' not to be appointed agents, realised it put the company at a disadvantage regarding its customers, who would all have to queue to pay once at Wembley. However, realising South Midland had limited vehicle resources at its disposal, decided that not only would they supply charabancs for private parties, but could take advantage of a larger fleet by offering from the opening of the BEE in April, a twice-a-week service departing Oxford at 09.00am returning 06.00pm. This did, however, necessitate the suspension of its express to Marble Arch.

City of Oxford continued the twice weekly service throughout the month of May but from June added a third day and changed the days from a Monday and Thursday to a Monday, Wednesday and Friday timings also changed Oxford departure 08.30am and return at 06.30pm from Wembley. Demand must have far exceeded supply at this point and with South Midland vehicles totally unable to cope with the numbers, Beesley probably approached COMS with an offer to supply exhibition entry tickets, in an effort to further increase SM ticket sales and revenue. However, this resulted in COMS being able to offer an all-inclusive fare to the exhibition of ten shillings. Obviously COMS management would have accepted the offer with open arms, as by now the time taken to gain entry once at Wembley must have been several hours on many occasions.

During early July the Company moved into larger premises at 111 St.Aldates, still in central Oxford. It should be noted that this was a short way from the garage premises at 5/6 Brewers Street where, since the Spring

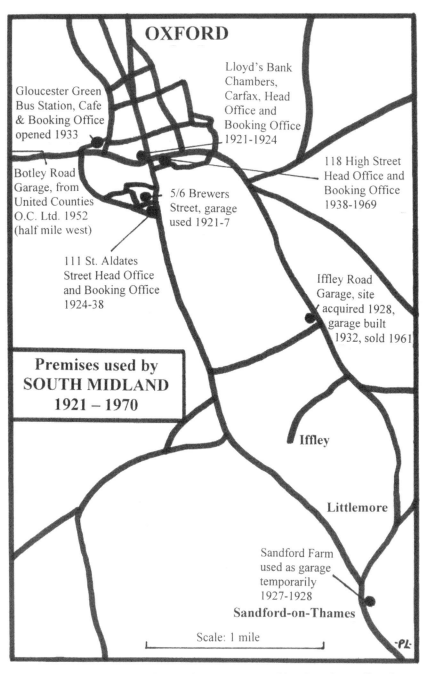

Sketch map of the relative locations used by South Midland.

of 1921 the small fleet of charabancs and lorries had been kept. Full use was made of this large shed and the yard with its lock-up garages, the latter being rented out. With sales of petrol and battery-charging for the public, the income generated helped subsidise SM's own requirements at the 'South Midland Garage'. The securing of such a central sites was no doubt of some significance in the Company's ability to attract sufficient trade, despite the City of Oxford company having a much larger charabanc fleet at its disposal.

Likewise, the extra shop space at St. Aldates was suitably occupied by yet another enterprise, with the 'South Midland Wireless Depot', which catered for another modern innovation of that age, with William Beesley as Managing Director! Later cigarette sales helped to bring the public into the shop and reduce overheads. Both the express service and excursions left from outside the Town Hall, just opposite the booking office, which was also convenient for supervision of departures.

With improved access to tickets, COMS advertised for July and August a service seven days a week to Wembley. Interestingly on five days a week the service journeyed via Headington, Stokenchurch and High Wycombe, on the other two days via Abingdon, Benson and Henley. For September the route returned to the June schedule of three days of the week, due I suspect to private hire commitments, using the new route via Stokenchurch and High Wycombe (by gentleman's agreement again?). Both companies now advertised a child fare of six shillings including admission, which again showed a strange lack of competition between the two concerns.

The difference the British Empire Exhibition made to South Midland cannot be overstated. It would be no exaggeration to say that as a result of the buoyant conditions it found itself in during 'twenty-four the company became firmly established, and also returned a healthy balance sheet, and probably wiping out all previous losses. As a direct result of the enhanced performance a dividend of two and a half per cent on total share capital was paid to the directors. It is in fact interesting to speculate just how much longer William Taylor might have been happy to bankroll the Company without some sort of return. My betting is that this could well have been regarded as the 'decision year' and had the tide not turned he would have called it a day and put it down to experience. So, when all's said and done, it seems that the might of the British Empire provided the very salvation that South Midland required to shake off its sometimes precarious start, not that all would be plain sailing from now on, as we shall soon see.

Chapter Five   Up's and Down's

The haulage operation received some attention, with the arrival in early October 1924 of an ex-WD Thornycroft J-type lorry repainted into a brown livery (FC 7333). This may have ousted the Hallford, which is not heard of again, and at least one more J-type was acquired in 1926, as were cars for hire. A daily run between Oxford and London was soon established.

1925 saw the company optimistic enough that in April a fifth vehicle joined the fleet, a move back to the Dennis marque with a faithful 2.5-ton chassis. Fitted with pneumatic tyres and also probably spring seats now very popular, it was registered FC 8130. The British Empire Exhibition would again dominate the vehicle loadings, though advertised tours equated to the use of two vehicles daily except on Saturdays, with typically a pattern of runs on Sundays and Thursdays to Southsea, plus a tour to Cheltenham and Birdlip, Mondays and Wednesdays to Stratford-on-Avon and a tour to Windsor and the Thames Valley and on a Tuesday, and on Friday a tour to the Berkshire Downs and a separate tour to the Savernake Forest. With the exception of Southsea at 07.30am, all were afternoon departures leaving Oxford at 02.30pm, many shops still having a half-day closing each week.

Representing the next stage of evolution of the motor coach was FC 8130, with its 'allweather' bodywork, central gangway and pneumatic tyres. This happy outing was from Littlemore to the popular resort of Southsea.

Towards London South Midland confirmed operations to Wembley from July to October inclusive, with daily service timings unchanged. However, with travel generally increasing enquiries for central London must have reached a new high, for during August and September the original Marble Arch route resumed, as an additional London service, again including the Zoo drop off point, timings unchanged from those previously set when last operated. As if again to try and be one jump ahead of expectations Wembley added another attraction a 'Torchlight Tattoo'. South Midland reacted by offering a 01.30pm lunch-time departure on a Thursday and Saturday to the Tattoo returning from Wembley at 10.00pm.

COMS treated Wembley more as a regular excursion in this year, surprising in some ways, as they had managed to be appointed BEE Official Agents in Oxford along with SM. However, maybe this led to increased private hire bookings to such a level that restrictions on the operation of any express type service to Wembley let alone Marble Arch was out of the question. The excursions to the exhibition ran two days each week in May, June and July, four days weekly in August and three days each week during September and October. The COMS answer to the 'Tattoo' spectacular was, perhaps surprisingly, a 'Long day at Wembley' which as suggested had the usual depart Oxford time of 08.30am return from Wembley at 10.00pm, hard on the poor driver, with all August to October Wembley excursions falling into this category!

Although as expected this had been a thoroughly satisfactory year for South Midland in terms of revenue, and for the country as a whole the British Empire Exhibition had been something of a morale booster, those lucky enough to visit were left generally very enthralled at what they had seen. However, dark clouds were gathering, the state of Britain was far from 'Great'. In nineteen twenty six the ramifications of the employment situation and working conditions generally was becoming only too obvious, South Midland one of probably thousands of businesses starting to reel from non-payment of invoices overdue from nineteen twenty five, or in other words an increasing number of bad debts.

Notwithstanding these eventually having to be written off, a small surplus was still made in 'twenty five, but in relation to all the sales that had been generated not the result Mr Beesley and Mr Taylor would have desired or even thought likely after the beginning of that year. Matters had taken a turn for the worse in nineteen twenty five when the mine-owners had announced that they intended to reduce the miners wages. However, with

Union intervention, the Conservative government of the day had supplied the mine owners with the necessary money to keep the miners pay at the same level thereby alleviating strike action, although the Prime Minister Stanley Baldwin had stated this was a temporary arrangement.

In March 1926, when the government money had ceased, the mine-owners gave notice that pay would be cut by twenty five per cent from the first of May. On this same day a General Strike was announced by the Trade Union Congress to commence the third of May, involving miners, railwaymen, transport workers, dockers, printers, builders and iron and steel workers, about a fifth of the adult working male population. Although the strike lasted only ten days before a general return to work, and certainly by the end of June industry (mine workers the exception) was back to some sort of normality, many employers used the situation to impose longer working hours on employees for lower wages.

It would be the October of this year before the miners began to drift back to work in any large numbers, and this due to the obvious hardships being felt by the families involved. From the South Midland perspective, or maybe it should be called the Oxford perspective and its subsequent effect on SM, it would be correct to say that my research through the local Oxford newspapers of the time show that the population of this city was very anti the General Strike. Many stories recalled in the newspapers illustrating this feeling, though much that was reported could have been editorial propaganda or selective reporting. However, it was alleged that when Union members tried to hold meetings to convince COMS employees to 'come out and support the cause', the response varied from vociferous heckling to downright hostility, one meeting in particular reported that representatives had to disappear quite rapidly fearing physical attack.

I am not convinced the view in Oxford was so clear cut for several reasons. In many areas of the country it can be confirmed from reading the various fleet histories that have been compiled, this particular strike, rather bizarre as it may seem was the making of many a passenger transport company. Perhaps the best known was Elliott Brothers of Bournemouth trading as 'Royal Blue', who found that business was suddenly generated to such a degree that on the route to London up to thirty coaches a day could be operating! South Midland who, on the other hand, had advertised their London (Marble Arch) service at the beginning of May nineteen twenty six, appear then to have suspended the service, possibly because of the perceived dangers of operating during the General Strike, given the alleged

31

attitude of Oxfordians to the action, but did not restart the service at all during the course of the year. It is logical to have expected SM to capitalise during this period if as a company they and its employees had been so against the strike as publicised.

The other view of course, whilst unlikely, given that South Midland employees at this point in time were probably all ex-servicemen for King and Country etc., is that this concern did have some sympathy for the miners cause. Bearing in mind that the miners themselves were a well respected bunch equal with servicemen, in that if you had been a miner when the war commenced in the dangerous conditions that were common then in the pits, an individual would have had no problem 'opting out' of war duty, although many did go and fight, as the profession was considered an essential service to keep the country going for the war effort. This viewpoint would also explain the postponement of the express service to London, and by October when the miners had officially returned to work, the express route season would have been at an end in any case.

The fact that COMS failed to resurrect its London service would of course been due to its stated position and that allegedly of its employees on the action taken by the Unions nationally, and its worry that reprisals might be forthcoming against its vehicles and employees on such journeys. Whatever version, COMS would never again ply the Oxford-London road with an express operation in its own name. South Midland continued to advertise a limited excursion programme, surprising given the fact that it now had additional vehicles available due to non-operation of the London service. However possibly private hire traffic was still being generated and may well have increased, due in part to a wider population having experienced SM first hand through the British Empire Exhibition. The traffic catchment area had also become enlarged as a result, added to which an ever increasing number of societies and clubs were showing a preference for charabancs when arranging outings, due to the flexibility over trains for instance. The AGM for this year did however report a falling off in fees for motor coaches, which provided yet another test for the Company.

One senses that the end of each charabanc 'season' saw a period of some reflection and planning for the forthcoming year at South Midland. However, with rapid improvements in vehicle design, the concept of all-year-round services was taking shape. The pioneer Bristol – London route of Greyhound Motors started the vogue for express coach service from its inception in February 1925 that would do much to shape SM's future.

Chapter Six   Towards Change

A general malaise seem to cover the country in nineteen twenty seven, and whatever your opinion of the industrial unrest the year previous much government propaganda was generated which was aimed to humiliate those that had taken part in the action. Some individuals had to eventually leave the country to find work abroad, as things would never be quite the same again. Obviously a very difficult time to try and judge the passenger transport market, and a much more business minded William Beesley would by now have become a more cautious individual. He had experienced both peaks and troughs, although not in that order, of the travel industry and probably felt this year would be difficult to forecast. It is perhaps with this in mind that South Midland chose not to pursue the London service in this year, though twice-weekly excursions were advertised to the Zoo on Monday and Thursday from May through to September. I am sure if enquiries had been such that a justification for the re-introduction of the express service could have been made it would have happened, or at least additional excursions advertised.

That this appeared to be the situation in Oxford was at odds to the picture nationally, with competition very much 'hotting up' in the country as a whole and notwithstanding Beesley's pioneering efforts in the field of express operation, this area of business now seemed to be rapidly increasing in this year. London seemed to be bearing the brunt of this explosion and along with a large increase in excursion traffic, at least that was the perception of Government, leading a spokesperson to state the situation was 'reaching levels of concern'. Operators were also trying to establish connecting points for through bookings, again notably to and from London and beyond, one of the early reputable operator organisations that of London Coastal Coaches.

By now this grouping consisted principally of Tilling, BAT (who later combined) and National Omnibus subsidiaries plus Elliott Brothers (still private at this point), plus Redcar Services who operated routes to the Tonbridge and Tunbridge Wells areas of Kent. Although no one arrival /departure location existed in London yet for this scheme, the benefits of being part of such an organisation soon came to the attention of William Beesley. Also William would have noticed the increase in advertised scheduled express services via Oxford suddenly hitting the local newspapers from the North West, Midlands and South Wales in particular, in their infancy just now, but about to gather momentum. Therefore mindful of all this and weighing up the pro's and con's of which direction to proceed, become an established express operator or rely predominately on private hire and excursion work as the main source of income.

Such decisions followed a little later and would not become apparent until the following year, as for now William was happy to bide his time and with private hire bookings which were extremely healthy in this year. In fact to quote from the AGM minutes 'a vast number of bookings and contracts have been obtained for nineteen twenty seven'. On 30th May it was announced that the lease on the premises in Brewers Street garage had run out, so temporary accommodation was arranged at Sandford Farm, 3 miles south of the city. Finally a sixth vehicle was added to the fleet in June of this year and broke new ground for South Midland in both vehicle type and specification. Registered WL 2696, it was a maroon-liveried Italian-built Lancia 'Pentaiota', with seating for twenty four and described as 'the latest type of luxury coach, incorporating separate seats with pneumatic upholstery, as used in private cars of the more expensive type, and fitted with heating for cold weather' - a precursor for a return to London runs?

Nineteen twenty eight saw confirmation of which direction in general South Midland were going to go and also illustrated William Beesley had been far from idle the year before. From the beginning of this year a daily service began between Oxford and London, very large advertisements being placed in the local press detailing the timed stops now, the departure times from these stops and the single and return fares from each place name. It was a brave move by SM to re-establish itself on that road, and Beesley would have been excused for stopping with private hire, excursion and contract work especially so given that the accounts for 'twenty-seven recorded increased earnings.

In order to address the longer-term need for garaging, another business that had originated in the early post-Great War years was acquired. 'Oxford Motor Carriers & Repairers Ltd.' had become established at 55 Magdalen Street by 1921, adding garage premises in Iffley Road by 1924. Motor haulage and general garage work were promoted side by side. The SM Board confirmed the acquisition at a Special Meeting on 7th July 1928.

To generate much additional traffic from the London end of the route, agreement had been reached with Charles Rickards Limited of Spring Street opposite Paddington Station, West London to act as agents. This explodes another myth that 'when this service was established in 1928 all passengers originated from Oxford as there were no agents' which has frequently been repeated. As if to epitomise the confidence that SM was now showing in its commitment to the London express service, no time was wasted in ordering two more Lancia's for the fleet. Obviously they were very pleased with the 24-seater already in service and the comments emanating from customers conveyed by this superior machine.

In February a Weymann-bodied twenty-six seater arrived registration WL 4131 followed in the May by the second vehicle WL 5055 seating this time twenty-eight. Whatever the previous book fleet numbers used, if any, this last Lancia commenced the official fleet numbering of the company when it became number 14. It is interesting to note that William Beesley's daughter informed me during my research, and a good while before I had amassed fleet vehicle details, that her Father had stated to her that when he had decided to use fleet numbers he had commenced at a high number. She was unable to recall the first number herself, though his principal reason for commencing the display of fleet numbers was to give the impression of a much larger fleet than was actually in existence - quite common at the time in fact. However, if that was indeed the reason, I am puzzled as to why, given the fleet strength, a much higher number was not chosen.

The second of the trio of Lancia Pentaiota 'allweather' coaches was this Weymann-bodied example (WL 4131), also in a maroon livery. The third of this type was, however, finished in a scheme of silver and maroon.

However, to confuse the issue even further in the July a fourteen-seater charabanc was acquired from the well known company of House Brothers of Watlington Oxfordshire. Registered BL 1351, it was a Hotchkiss chassis originating in 1914 as a 4-seater car. Somewhat of a mystery surrounds this vehicle, which did not receive a fleet number. House as an operator seems to have gone from strength to strength over the years from this point in time, it was either a vehicle purchased when that Company's finances were not at their best or from an operational perspective found to have insufficient capacity. Although it obviously fitted into South Midland's requirements at that precise moment of time, probably for more small-party traffic such as sports teams, its stay was rather short with disposal around October 1928. Whilst with SM it ran in a silver and maroon livery.

Due to the engineering advances now taking place within the passenger chassis market, the journey time to London was now three hours departing Oxford at 08.30am arriving Marble Arch at 11.30am returning from London at 06.30pm, giving passengers seven hours in the Capital. Fares charged were ten shillings return the single fare six shillings and sixpence, although from Dorchester and Henley for example you would have paid nine shillings and five shillings and sixpence and seven shillings and three shillings and sixpence respectively - the Henley figure striking me as very competitively priced.

I have mentioned competition was ever increasing on the Oxford to London corridor albeit if only by services going through Oxford en route to or from destinations further afield, it was the aim of course of these operators to abstract as much traffic from South Midland as possible. Although through their experience of travelling by SM from the early days and in no uncertain terms the reputation of Beesley himself, noted as a fair and just individual and employer, many an Oxford citizen religiously travelled by 'his' South Midland, but there were still many who were not in a financial position to remain loyal when the competition in this year were offering a wider choice of services at lower fares.

The main protagonists in the war for passengers from and to Oxford appearing in this year were Grays, trading as Red & Black, based in Tottenham North London (although operating from the Aldwych in Central London), and Samuelson Saloon Coaches operating from their base at Victoria in London. These companies had effectively chosen to 'blitz' the route, Red & Black alternating journeys to Oxford to run either via High Wycombe or via Maidenhead and Henley, with six journeys daily Monday to Saturday and three journeys on a Sunday. In addition a Thursday only service departing Oxford at 02.00pm returning from London at 11.30pm operated for the benefit of theatregoers. To add insult to injury during the first months of operation children twelve years of age or under accompanying a fare-paying adult travelled free! Ground breaking also at the time, this company had found a legal loophole to alleviate advanced booking by issuing tickets on the coach avoiding the regulations by a minimum threepence fare. Samuelson's for their part were offering five daily journeys either routed by way of High Wycombe or Thame using four local Oxford booking agents, the main one being C. Taphouse and Son of Magdalen Street.

Such an onslaught would indeed require a man of nerves of steel at the helm of South Midland, and as can be seen over and over again Beesley just seemed to take it all in his stride. As we have also seen he had an uncanny knack for seizing an opportunity should it arise and with most of the routes north, west and east out of Oxford being 'over serviced' by operators, it was only natural Beesley looked south. Here he observed The Link Safety Coach Company operating a new service between Oxford and Bournemouth via Reading with no competition yet visible. He made immediate arrangements with that Company to act as their Oxford booking agents, the Link service itself continued from Oxford to Birmingham, in fact the coach heading south would meet with the coach going north at Oxford and both would then depart on their respective ways at 01.30pm.

Nineteen twenty-nine was to be a significant year in the history of road passenger transport. The government had a view that disorder, bordering on anarchy, existed in bus and coach operation in general and in London particularly, and that State intervention was necessary in the industry. An oft-quoted example of this, though by no means unique, was the Cambridge - London service, where the price war between the two main operators having reached the absurd level whereby Varsity Express Motors and Westminster Coaching Services had reduced prices to a return fare of two shillings - but which probably fatally wounded both concerns. The situation resulted in a Royal Commission of nineteen twenty nine being set up to look at the problems, which in turn would lead to the Road Traffic Act of nineteen thirty, although it would be April nineteen thirty one before it became truly effective. However, the writing was already on the wall, during which time the industry would be completely turned up on its head, although I will cover the detail of the act in the next chapter.

To try and rebuff the competition an increase in the number of journeys between Oxford and London was imperative. As this would need much additional capital specifically to increase the coach fleet, William turned his attention to the builder that had, the previous year, completed a new house for his family and himself in Summertown a growing suburb of Oxford. This gentleman one Harry Capon, and due no doubt to the powers of

37

persuasion used by Beesley at which he was very adept. He advanced a considerable sum as a debenture to South Midland and this, along with additional guarantees from current directors, enabled orders to be placed for four new vehicles.

Possibly due to delivery constraints, the order was split, three Dennis coaches and one Gilford. Initially a Dennis G chassis had been ordered, but as the model had been superceded by the GL type, one was taken instead and fitted with Arnold and Comben twenty-seater bodywork being delivered in the May as fleet number 15 (WL 7221). Two of the larger Dennis F types became fleet numbers 16/7 (WL 7240/7456) and received twenty-eight seat bodies again by Arnold and Comben, the latter chassis numbered 80104 being the very last F type built, and both of these vehicles appeared in the June. The Gilford, which was yet again bodied by A & C - this bodybuilder being exclusively used for orders from then until the end of nineteen thirty - also arrived in the May of this year along with the GL previously mentioned. Although other Gilford's would be ordered into the beginning of the next decade, this vehicle would be unique in the fleet as the only normal-control example, becoming No.18 (WL7233).

In yet another step towards the zenith of coaching luxury, the low-slung F-type Dennis chassis, with well-appointed Arnold & Comben bodywork went a long way to securing South Midland's popularity for passenger comfort.

With the new vehicles on board, and being able now to boast a fleet of thirteen vehicles, from May the daily departures from Oxford to London

38

became 09.00am, 02.30pm and 06.30pm and from London to Oxford at 09.30am, 02.30pm and 06.30pm, with the return fare unchanged at ten shillings but the single reduced by sixpence to six shillings. In a new innovation, for South Midland at least, children would travel at half price. Excursions were completely rejuvenated over the summer in this year also, Southsea for example operating every Tuesday, Thursday, Saturday plus on

WL 7456 was the second of the F-types, and in fact the last of that type to be built. The pair were finished in another new livery of cream and red.

Sundays over the holiday season. Five excursions were advertised daily consisting of one all day and four afternoon tours. The revised express service led to the outstationing of a coach in London, probably at Rickards.

Evidently impressed at the success the Link Safety Coach Company was having with its Bournemouth - Birmingham via Reading and Oxford route, a tentative agreement was made by SM to take over the company and assume its liabilities, issuing to the partners Mr P A Parkes and Mr A Douch as purchase consideration five hundred ordinary shares each and to employ both individuals at a rate of £260 per annum. Whatever happened regarding the deal, which appeared *fait accompli*, is a complete mystery, insofar as research has revealed no valid reason why what appears to be a 'done deal' appears to fade into oblivion. However, South Midland had commenced an Oxford to Bournemouth service on 1st June 1929, departing Oxford at 09.00am returning from Bournemouth at 06.00pm, advertised as in conjunction with Link and operating via Reading also, and Beesley's daughter remembers travelling on this service several times on SM vehicles, so one assumes there had been no great falling out with the Link proprietors. Indeed, the SM coach left the Bournemouth end from Link's premises at Lansdowne Road, which only adds to the mystery.

One theory centres on a COMS advert on 28th June 1929 announcing a once daily service to Bournemouth departing Oxford 12.50pm but taking the more direct route via Newbury, Winchester and Southampton, followed by an express service on the Birmingham section primarily aimed again at Link departing Oxford at 03.15pm. Although purporting to being local in origin, it soon became apparent that operation was actually by Midland Red. Beesley appreciated the ramifications of taking that large concern on, probably resulting in his withdrawal from the planned purchase of Link. Control of Link duly passed to Black & White (in which both Midland Red and City of Oxford were of course shareholders) in late 1932, who finally absorbed them on behalf of Associated Motorways in May 1933.

During 1929 quite a lot of money was spent on the Iffley Road site, which was situated just south of the junction with Addison Crescent. The finance for this work and, in due course, the planned coach garage, came from Clara McCubbin. However, there were some reservations regarding the viability of the garage business, now known as the 'South Midland Garage' and including an Essex car agency, leading to the suggestion of forming it into a separate business to facilitate ease of disposal if required.

Finally to end the decade, which had seen South Midland rise from obscurity to become a well respected established local concern, the accounts for this year were quoted as 'highly satisfactory', which seems a just and fitting end to this period. However, competition was emerging in the form of Varsity Express Motors, with 4 daily departures Monday to Saturday between Oxford and London 07.30am, 10.30am, 01.30pm and 06.30pm and on Sundays two departures 08.15am and 06.15pm in the autumn of this year - all timed to compete with SM departures from London at similar timings. To make matters worse the return fare was six shillings and sixpence, a full third less than SM, and four shillings and sixpence single, also a reduction of approximately twenty five per cent over SM. Although this service operated via High Wycombe, Uxbridge and Southall to London, with such a dramatic reduction in through fares, Beesley had no choice but to reduce SM fares accordingly to match the Varsity pricing which he did in the October of this year. To have ignored this situation would have been to put all the hard work to date in jeopardy.

Chapter Seven   The Road Traffic Act 1930

1930 would indeed be a vintage year one way and another, due to the upheaval about to be 'thrust' upon the industry and the uncertainties of how the situation might effect each and every one of the operators involved. Many of them, like South Midland, were a small business compared to the large combines that were starting to loom large like preying mantises, buying up right, left and centre. This is at least how many of the operators would view the impending changes, many deciding to retire from passenger transport, whilst others considered they had built up a reasonably good business which must have some worth, and would offer to sell their Company to a neighbouring large operator. Because of the new licensing procedure about to 'kick in', these would be considered carefully by those larger operators who might very well decide to purchase, seeing the move as a shrewd investment.

In truth there was no exact science on how best to react to the proposed legislation, and those that for one reason or another found themselves having to press ahead and make applications. Although an unknown experience at the time, they would find out that indeed the necessity to hold such a license would, if granted, add value to the business eventually. On the other hand the owners of these companies could spend much time and money in court battles in the future, if a policy of expansion was planned, and very often without any return for their endeavours. Before setting out the basics of the legislation, it needs to be understood that capacity in the industry far exceeded requirement by 1930 and operators everywhere were beginning to feel the strain. As Garcke's 'Motor Transport Year Book' reported, in the 14 years from 1916 the numbers in the industry had swollen from 331 to almost 4000. To take Oxford as an example, as this history has illustrated at the start of the story in the early 'twenties, just 2 operators plied the road to London each operating 1 service daily. By 1930 this had grown to 18 express operators running 25 routes into / out of Oxford to London, with a total of 58 daily services in operation. As implied the majority of these services commenced many miles from Oxford, however the companies involved would be only too happy to convey traffic originating locally to the ultimate destination of the particular service in London.

The basis of the Road Traffic Act 1930, as envisaged by the Government of the day, was to bring some semblance of order out of the perceived chaos that bus and coach operations were in. The act required any operator wishing to provide a regular service that would be advertised to the general public to have a licence, although the service may already be operating or established for some time. The licence applied for would stipulate route, picking up and setting down points, a time and fare table and the maximum number of vehicles to be operated. Objectors to a published application could be other operators, railways, police or local authorities or other interested parties. Any bus or coach service, excursions and extended tours would all come under the legislation. Along with the Act also came Drivers Hours Regulations, no longer would bus or coach drivers be allowed to work for as long as their employers desired, though one obvious benefit announced was the increase in speed allowed for passenger service vehicles to a maximum of 30 miles per hour.

The system was to be administered by part-time Traffic Commissioners and a full time Chairman by means of Public Hearings, decisions taken at these could be appealed against by the operators concerned. In the case of long-distance express services, the Act had probably not been sufficiently vetted, as it was not long before major operators, including members of the umbrella Associated Motorways, started to bring in legal arguments that had to be thoroughly tested to become case law judgements. These were mainly concerning 'backing licenses' to cover long-distance routes running through several (or more) Traffic Areas, many of which were, needlessly, objected to by local concerns that had no real interest in those passengers.

One of the other operators through Oxford in 1929 was Great Western Express, brainchild of Gerald Nowell, who we shall hear more of later on. This 1929 Leyland Tiger TS2 (MT 2049) ran to Neath via Gloucester.

Chapter Eight   The New Order

To get back on track with South Midland, the garage subsidiary operating as South Midland Garages at the Iffley Road site, was not producing the required return and in March 1930 was sold to City Motor Company (Oxford) Limited for £5,200, so that SM could concentrate on its core business of coaching. Lockups on the site were not included in the transaction, but were rented to City Motors and a shop that was also part of the property was also rented out, to a C G Chaplin. March also saw the nominal capital of the Company increased to £10,000 by issue of £4000 in additional ordinary shares and £3000 of preference shares.

For some inexplicable reason from the January to the March of this year, all departures of SM commenced from the car park at St Aldates, one possible reason could have been that building works were taking place at Gloucester Green, although SM would continue to be the only operator for some time to come to describe Gloucester Green as the cattle market, notwithstanding this was its function, but from a public relations viewpoint the mental picture portrayed by either description of this site would indeed conjure up completely opposite visions of your departure point. South Midland in this year were now working in conjunction with London Coastal Coaches, the most obvious change being that SM coaches London arrival/departure point was now at 1a Lupus Street near Vauxhall Bridge, a rather bleak location, without cover and seemingly the hub of chaos.

However this was still a significant move, as the majority of independents were consigned to the rival Central London Coaching Station, which although considered superior in many respects, used by the likes of Greyhound of Bristol fast establishing a fine reputation in the express market. Although a covered location, the venue would however have an extremely limited life span, whereas within a few years a new state of the art coach station in Victoria would replace Lupus Street, giving SM the full benefit of the facilities offered, and also make South Midland unique amongst other users in being the only small independent authorised to use the coach station - a not to be under estimated achievement for such a business!

New vehicles started to arrive in the February and would continue to do so until August of this year. A total of 9, they were a combination of forward-control Gilford 168OT chassis and Arnold & Comben bodies, with varying seating capacities from 28 to 32 in number, all front entrance and carrying

43

fleet numbers 19 through to 27 These would be the last vehicles delivered to the South Midland Transport and Touring Company, and were registered in fleet number order as WL 9058, WL 9076, WL 9079, WL 9081, WL 9415, WL 9810, WL 9862 and JO 200 – no doubt the spread of those numbers pleased William Beesley, as it implied there were far more vehicles than actually so!

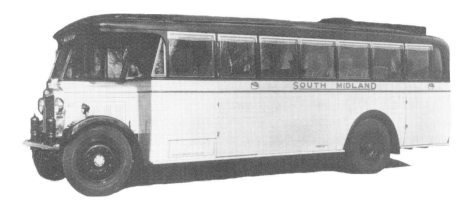

Gilford No.20 (WL 9076) in the view used for South Midland publicity. These coaches were finished in a scheme of cream and dark red like the 1929 Dennis and Gilford coaches from the same Farnham coachbuilder.

At the beginning of January in this year, Varsity had changed some of its London express service timings and added an extra journey, the Oxford daily departures now 07.30am, 08.35am, 10.30am, 02.00pm and 06.15pm, London departures at 10.30am, 01.30pm, 04.30pm, 06.30pm and 09.00pm (NS) or 11.30pm (Sat), whilst Sunday times were unchanged. A peculiarity at this point in time was the requirement on a Wednesday each week to vacate Gloucester Green for market day and remove the setting down point to elsewhere in the centre of the city. It can only be assumed that the individual places chosen by the various operators were conveyed to the general public when booking a ticket if your departure date was on this day of the week, but Varsity throughout all their publicity made a point of informing all of those concerned on this particular day the pick up/set down point was St Giles, and I think this was probably the same location for all operators, but a nice touch in customer relationships.

It was not until the beginning of April that the new improved South Midland timetable became operative, by which time probably five of the new Gilford's were in use. Quite dramatic changes were involved on the London express service which was now increased from three to six journeys daily, from Oxford at 09.00am, 10.15am, 12.30pm, 02.15pm, 05.00pm and 07.00pm, from London at 09.00am, 10.30am, 12.30pm, 02.15pm, 05.30pm and 07.30pm. Great play was made of the London Coastal Coaches association, although curiously not by name, but by the emphasis that 'These services make a direct connection in London with all the principal coach services in Britain and through tickets are issued by South Midland'.

Seen at Gloucester Green is Gilford No.19 (WL 9058) on the new service to Worcester, some 56 miles north-west of Oxford. Note the older Lancia all-weather coach still in use on the right.

Also commencing at the same date was a new Oxford to Worcester service departing Oxford twice a day at 11.45am and 05.15pm and at this point in time I believe, by the advertising and times of the London – Oxford departures, this service was altogether a separate departure situation. In addition to City of Oxford Motor Services advertising as booking agents for Midland Red, North Western and Majestic services to London, under those respective companies names now, it was also detailing extra journeys on this trunk road by Greyhound, for which they were also the acting agents at its 138 High Street office. An interesting innovation, which I could not find repeated elsewhere in Oxford, was that offered by Bells Travel Bureau, which for passengers booking a motor coach journey at their agency, offered one hundred pounds worth of travel insurance free, and it is of interest that their large advertisement featured a drawing of a Dennis F type identical to that operated by SM but minus any fleet name.

Although Varsity had fired the first salvo of increased journeys to London in the January of this year, still using Regent Street as the set down pick up point, which would continue to generate traffic for those simply wishing to travel to London, and arguably such a central point could appear much more attractive than Vauxhall to would be travellers, it had probably second guessed that SM would turn up the heat at the start of the April season, which as mentioned it duly did. So from this date it also upped the stakes by adding another three journeys, only retaining the Oxford departure times of 07.30am, 08.35am and 06.15pm, the remaining five re-timings and extra services departing Oxford 10.35am, 01.35pm, 2.35pm, 4.35pm and a new later 08.00pm, those ex-London introducing a new earlier departure at 09.15am, plus additional timings of 11.30am and 07.30pm. Sunday services were increased to four journeys each way, from Oxford extra timings of 10.00am and 08.00pm and from London 09.45am and 07.30pm. This timetable introduced a new slogan by Varsity 'Insist on Travelling by Varsity Express Motors Limited' (capital letters used as per original advertisement).

During the Easter period SM did operate 8 excursions, including to Newbury Races which was becoming a favourite now with the public, but was dwarfed by the large number of excursions advertised by COMS which illustrated the different directions both companies were now taking, this type of work and stage carriage for COMS, SM undertaking express work, occasional excursion and private hire bookings. However, it must be said that from the April COMS now had an indirect interest in express operation, since their purchase from the Birmingham & Midland Motor Omnibus Co Ltd (Midland Red) of a 20% share of Black & White Motorways, BMMO having purchased B & W for £100,000 on the 30th April, Bristol Tramways & Carriage Company also having a 40% stake. Greyhound had decided to increase its Gloucester to London service via Oxford to 5 journeys daily, however obviously receiving a 'bloody nose' early on in terms of passenger numbers, but retreated fairly fast as the additional services lasted some 6 weeks. May saw the re-introduction of the daily Southsea service by SM, leaving Oxford at 08.00am and 01.30pm whilst in June South Midland amended its London express timetable to incorporate an early departure from Oxford and a late departure from London at 07.15am and Midnight respectively, probably based on observations by William Beesley of loadings on the Varsity first Oxford departure and demand from the public (I would assume theatre goers) for a later time from the capital.

During June many more excursions were listed by South Midland, not that any new tours appeared from that advertised in previous years, although obviously still very popular. I suspect the delay was due to awaiting the completion of the order for Gilford chassis, the early deliveries being required for the expanded express services. That month saw the Oxford-Worcester route receive time changes, departing Oxford now at 12.00 noon and 06.00pm which would again be changed on Saturday the 9th August to 11.45am and 05.45pm, this last change I believe, due to this route becoming at that point a London-Oxford-Worcester daily service, both timings and service remaining unchanged for the rest of the year. The surprise of June in this year had to be the introduction of the Oxford-Nottingham via Leicester express service by SM, with departures from Oxford at 08.30am and 05.30pm, could this have been to test the traffic volumes before route applications were submitted. This service had time revisions from Saturday 2nd August the early departure withdrawn, replaced by a 03.30pm timing, yes that's right two departures two hours apart, however the service only continued until mid October before withdrawal.

A merry party from Littlemore about to take to the seaside on the Gilford normal-control coach No.18 (WL 7233) and one of the forward-control examples delivered in 1930. Beesley had connections with the area, leading to the regular use of South Midland coaches for village outings.

South Midland carried out two more sets of time changes before the year end to fine tune the service for customers. During July when the Sunday timetable to London from Oxford was altered to a five times a day service 08.00am, 10.15am, 12.30pm, 02.15pm and 07.00pm., and from the beginning of November, when the revamp saw the midnight service dropped from London and new ex London times of 09.00am, 10.30am, 01.30pm, 03.0 pm, 05.30pm, 07.30pm and 09.00pm. to Oxford. Surprisingly the Southsea route was operated daily through to the year-end, the only variation being that the early journey from Oxford ceased at the end of November leaving only the lunchtime service. Varsity for their part had only seen fit to implement one further change to remain competitive, and that was during August, when Sunday services were increased from four to six journeys the extra departures from Oxford 02.30pm and 09.00pm and from London 02.30pm and 10.30pm, however the 07.30pm from London was brought forward to leave at 06.30pm.

During September SM tried to gain another foothold by applying for a local Hackncy Carriage license from Reading Borough Council for the operation of an Oxford – Reading route. The purpose of this action was undoubtably to allow the Company to claim an existing service when the Act came into force, but the application was duly rejected on the basis that the existing long-established TV/COMS bus links at Wallingford were adequate.

Finally to end 1930, on the 25th October a Special Meeting was convened by special resolution, to change the name of the Company to South Midland Motor Services Limited, this name duly being registered exactly one month later on the 25th November. At the same meeting it was noted the accounts for the year were highly satisfactory, which implied this was the best years trading to date for SM, but I've no doubt this position owed much to the London Coastal Coaches connection, and again it has to be said that the foresight of Beesley in cultivating this association says much of the man and his entrepreneurial skills.

As 1931 dawned the industry in general was now in a very precarious state, and as it would turn out the implementation of the Road Traffic Act in this year would, in general, become a 'life saver', this not by design we know, nevertheless as is often the situation an outsiders viewpoint, the Government's in this case, can distinguish the wood from the trees, and although legislation came about more from the perception of what was happening in London, many of the constituent parts of that deemed problem were indeed endemic of the industry as a whole throughout the length and breadth of the country.

Life prior to the full implementation of the Act went on, and South Midland had continued to operate the Southsea service throughout the winter period, possibly to strengthen support for the applications the company was soon to make. The Worcester via Oxford to London twice a day service had also continued to run over the same period, fares for both SM and Varsity were now at five shillings single, seven shillings day return and eight shillings and sixpence period return.

For this year SM had departed from the Gilford make and had ordered four Leyland 'Tiger' TS3's, a model rapidly becoming very popular and no doubt had caught the eye of William Beesley as many of them came through Oxford run by competitors, and he would no doubt have overheard conversations of the coach drivers on a journey break discussing the merits of the various models, this being the drivers current favourite. The 'Tigers' carried fleet numbers 28-31 (JO 1597/9/3/5 – note the use of alternate numbers, albeit out of sequence!). The bodywork was another departure, being built by the London firm of Scammell & Nephew, with a 28-seat central entrance specification fitted with a superior type of upholstery. Two of the vehicles arrived in the March and two in the April, which fortuitously coincided with the season start at Easter, this saw South Midland only offer 3 full day and 10 half day excursions over the 4- day holiday period, compared with COMS offering 20 full day excursions.

Leyland 'Tiger' TS3 No.28 (JO 1597) as new, complete with route boards for the proposed Coventry service. These were well-appointed vehicles and quite an investment for South Midland. However, the bodies were not as well constructed as the chassis, resulting in their re-bodying in 1936.

On the 20th March of this year the following applications appeared in 'Notices and Proceedings' under the South Midland name, again citing the Cattle Market as the Oxford pick up point, the application details and numbers were as follows:-

J73-London to Worcester-Daily-Ex London times 10.00am and 03.00pm-Ex Worcester times 09.15am and 04.00pm- Objectors COMS plus three others.

J74-Oxford to Southsea – Daily April to September - Ex Oxford times 08.00am, 01.00pm and 05.30pm-Ex Southsea times 08.15am, 01.00pm and 06.00pm-Objectors GWR plus four others.

J75-Oxford to London – Daily – Ex Oxford times 07.15am (NSu), 08.00am (SSu), 09.00am (NSu), 10.00am, 11.00am (NSu), 12.15pm, 02.00pm, 04.00pm, 05.30pm (NSu), 06.30pm, 07.30pm and 08.00pm (SSu) – Ex London times 09.00am, 10.00am, 11.00am, 12.00noon (NSu), 02.00pm, 03.00pm, 04.00pm (NSu), 05.30pm, 07.30pm, 09.00pm and 12.00 midnight (SSu) - Objectors GWR plus four others

J76-Southsea to Worcester – Daily April to September – Ex Southsea times 08.15am and 01.00pm – Ex Worcester times 09.15am – Objectors GWR plus five others.

J77-Southsea to Coventry – Daily April to September – Ex Southsea times 08.15am and 01.00pm – Ex Coventry times 09.30am

J78-London to Coventry – Daily – Ex London times 09.00am and 02.00pm – Ex Coventry times 09.30am and 04.30pm.

All were listed for hearing on the 8th June, although somewhat unexplained, a note was added that J77 and J78 were not listed to be heard, I will make mention of this later. On the 19th June applications J73 through to J76 inclusive were granted and these four routes would be the basis of SM express services for the next forty years. Excursion applications followed later, quite why they were not included in the initial application I have no idea, but in N & P number eighteen dated the 17th July they duly appeared, being granted in full on the ninth of October as application **J1873** and consisted of the following destinations:- half day excursions Burnham Beeches, Berkshire Downs, Bibury and Cirencester, Windsor and Thames Valley, Chiltern Hills and Pangbourne, six in total; full day excursions Bournemouth, Bognor Regis, Southsea, Brighton, Bath and Bristol and Cheddar Caves, Shakespeare Country, Wye Valley, Malvern Hills, Weymouth, Weston-super-Mare, Southampton, Newbury Races, Ascot Races and Epsom Races, fourteen in total; and finally two evening only destinations were included to Aldershot Tattoo and Tidworth Tattoo.

A note stated that other excursions that arose through special occasions could also be operated, and that authorisation covered the operating at anytime between Easter and 30th September as long as no more than twenty vehicles were used in one day to cover such operations. The Varsity applications, worthy of mention as the main competitor to SM, did not appear in N & P until the 7th August and therefore correspondingly did not get granted until the 2nd October 1931. The application for the London express was numbered J2170 that for the excursions J2171 both obviously made at the same time. All listed Gloucester Green (SM's Cattle Market) as the Oxford pick up point, and it was surprising they had applied for excursions, as this side of the business never showed itself as operating previously, and even more unexpectedly they were granted. Details of the Road Service Licenses granted to Varsity are as follows:-

J2170-Oxford to London – Daily – Ex Oxford times Mon to Sat 07.30am, 08.35am, 09.35am, 10.35am, 01.35pm, 02.35pm, 04.35pm, 06.15pm and 08.00pm. Ex London times Mon to Sat 09.15am, 10.30am, 11.30am, 01.30pm, 02.30pm, 04.30pm, 06.30pm, 07.30pm (NTh), 09.00pm (NS) and 11.45pm(ThS) – Ex Oxford times on Sunday 08.15am, 10.00am, 02.35pm, 06.15pm, 08.00pm and 09.15pm. – Ex London times on Sunday 09.45am, 10.45am, 02.30pm, 06.30pm, 09.00pm and 10.30pm – Objectors GWR plus one other.

J2171-Excursions - Full day Ascot Races, Eastbourne, Epsom Races, Brighton, Hastings, Folkestone, Stratford-upon-Avon and London (as a day tour), eight in total, plus one evening excursion to Aldershot Tattoo. Authorisation was for anytime between 1st May and 30th September with a maximum authorised of twelve coaches in one day.

Concerning the Coventry express applications which were not heard at the Assembly Rooms, Oxford on the 8th June, the logic behind such services could not be questioned and it really defies belief such a service had not been tried several years previous by SM. Given that the route was via Warwick, Stratford–upon–Avon and Woodstock, not only extremely popular tourist areas, but destinations William Beesley had ensured his coaches visited on a fairly regular basis. Both the Coventry-London and seasonal Coventry-Southsea would of course have just been extensions of Oxford to London and Southsea routes in the same way as the respective Worcester services to the same destinations, the idea so simple one is at pains to know why its proposed operation only reared its head when making the formal application for services. Certainly Beesley was extremely confident for some reason, as the first Leyland 'Tiger' delivered

No.28 arriving in the March displayed roof-mounted sideboards proclaiming the service in very large capitals, and very smart it looked. However, I can find no record of the route being operated in the run-up period to the granting of the SM licences, and my only assumption can be that with the success Elliott Brothers (Royal Blue) were having in the express service field, having since 1929 operating a Bournemouth-Oxford-Coventry-Birmingham route, words were exchanged between the two companies and William Beesley decided not to pursue the application.

As I see it SM had nothing to lose, they did not have to appeal if the routes had not been granted and probably the lack of pursuit was part of a much bigger picture, one of which a fully satisfactory answer cannot be provided unfortunately. Was it tied in with the London Coastal Coaches connection, or was there a veiled threat of a counter application to established SM routes by Elliott's, although the chance of success for such applications would have been minimal. Whatever then full background, the photographs

This other view of No.28, again with boards for the Coventry route, was used in an advert by the manufacturer of the patent soundproof flooring!

of No.28 would come back to haunt Beesley for a while to come, as this particular vehicle would be depicted in several manufacturer advertisements at least up until the end of this year and into the next, as these things do. I wonder how many people having seen the picture might have been prompted to call into the SM office or telephone South Midland for details of this non-existent route! Last but not least, we must note that the accounts were still looking healthy despite significant fleet expansion, and also being set against the background of a deepening general depression in the country at large.

Chapter Nine   The Uneasy Peace

Into 1932 most operators were probably wondering what all the fuss had been about surrounding the new licensing system, those of course who had their applications granted in full, or the majority of the application granted. The results of the applications had, generally speaking, turned out to be fair, and as stated at the time if you had operated a route for the period stipulated, no problems generally had been encountered, 'grandfather rights' applying although not described as such. At least the industry now had some sort of disciplines in place.

Easter in this year for South Midland kicked in with the Southsea route commencing with just the 08.30 am and 01.30 pm departures from Oxford and it would not be until the beginning of July that the third departure time as granted on this licence would operate and only then until the end of August. However this first operation of the route post-Road Traffic Act amazingly saw, as already indicated, all departures from Oxford leaving thirty minutes later than originally applied for, also the first two departures from Southsea leaving fifteen minutes and thirty minutes later respectively than applied for. Around this time SM also secured contracts with the Cunard Line and Canadian Pacific to be able to offer the inbound tourists the opportunity to visit Oxford, Blenheim Palace and Stratford-on-Avon then to London over two days. That type of business fitted in very well with the other SM operations and through this connection it proved possible to advertise the occasional excursion to Southampton in that year which included the a *'Tour of inspection of the Giant Cunard Liner 'Mauretania' by courtesy of the Cunard Steamship Company'* - again as quoted in the SM literature, using capitals as used in the advertisements.

Other ships would also be included on various dates such as the 'Aquitania' and 'Berengaria', those three ships forming the backbone of the Cunard Line. Two of the three had four funnels each, the 'Berengaria' having three funnels and being an ex-German ship, all of them coming to the end of their useful life. The 'Mauretania' though held the infamous Blue Ribbon award for the fastest Atlantic crossing right up until 1929 and was therefore a special favourite. At a return fare of ten shillings being charged, with children at half price, the trip represented good value.

The Dennis GL 20-seater No.15 (WL 7221) departed in April 1932 whilst SM's only example of the improved Leyland 'Tiger' TS4 was delivered in

53

The Leyland 'Tiger' TS4 coach appeared on the literature of the period, wearing the red and cream livery in use at that time. The integral front destination and fleetname apertures and side panel for route description were standard Harrington features, as was the optional sliding roof panels.

54

June and bore fleet number 32 (JO 4789). It also broke new ground in being bodied by Harrington of Hove, and although it had obviously been planned to continue with Scammell & Nephew, as SM had options on eight more bodies, problems were already being encountered with their construction leading to the change. The relationship between Mr Harrington and William Beesley however was to blossom to more than placing orders for coach bodies, as they obviously got on so well that Beesley's daughter remembers spending much time at the Harrington family home on visits, the invitation being reciprocated at Williams' Summertown residence. Given the size of the SM fleet and the fact that only fourteen bodies in total over an eight year period would ever be ordered by the company during William Beesleys reign, this is proof if it were needed, that the relationship was more on a personal level between the families than a business one.

The body on the 'Tiger' TS4 was of the rear-entrance type with seating for thirty two. The vehicle also featured 'Greenline' style roof-mounted boards, but this time no mistakes were made, as the legend was for a route that really existed, being the regular London – Oxford - Worcester express service, those main place names in very large capitals. Six intermediate stops were named in smaller capitals, and the sideboard in this instance was built into the body itself and possibly even illuminated. To my mind this was the most attractive of all the South Midland vehicles to be delivered pre-war, a picture of the coach understandably appeared on the front of all the SM timetables until 1936.

South Midland changed the London - Oxford express times also in June, in what would be a milestone in the company's history, as the timings would not be varied at any time again from either end of the journey from this point on up until World War Two was declared. The new timetable was as follows, from Oxford 07.15am (NSu), 08.00am (Su), 09.00am (NSu), 10.15am, 12.30pm, 02.15pm, 05.00pm (NSu), 07.00pm, the 12.30pm and 07.00pm departures emanating from Worcester. From London 09.00am, 10.30am, 01.30pm (NSu), 03.00pm, 05.30pm (NSu), 07.30pm and 09.00pm, the 09.00am and 03.00pm Worcester bound. Varsity made a move, again in the June, which appeared insignificant at the time but was to prove important, when a small cabin was placed by the Company at Gloucester Green to accommodate bookings for its London express service. Finally, the South Midland accounts for the third year in a row were again very satisfactory, to be expected on the one hand given the consolidation now taking place within the Company, but slightly surprising giving the continuing decline of the prosperity of the country as a whole.

However, in 1933 with the depression becoming more acute, it was not only a necessity for SM to ensure maximum utilisation of its fleet as far as possible but also to find ways to generate more income. With the SM fleet larger than that of Varsity now, that operator did not pose a particular threat, although an eye needed to be kept on that business at all times. It was during such checks on the opposition that William Beesley noted that loadings had increased marginally on the Varsity routes, no particular timing or day of the week, just a gut feeling that during the latter part of 'thirty two Varsity loadings appeared a little better overall.

When reflecting on this, William decided it must be down to the booking office erected the previous year by Varsity at the coach departure point that went almost unnoticed at the time. However, it was now contributing to the Varsity 'coffers' by virtue of the fact would-be passengers were turning up at Gloucester Green to catch a coach, not having booked in advance, or wishing to go into the city for a ticket, and coming across the more conveniently situated Varsity office.

With this in mind, a tenancy agreement was made with Oxford Corporation for an office at Gloucester Green at a rent of £36 per annum. However, with the start of the year usually being slow business wise, it was decided to wait until the high season before opening, as a consequence was not open for trading until the 19th June. This had been something of a wake up call for William Beesley, as he realised he needed to get back into his old ways which had usually seen him ahead of the opposition in many respects. No doubt he felt that Varsity had ever so slightly caught him napping, perhaps due to pre-occupation with the work caused by the1930 Act?

In May an agreement was entered into to rent the Old Settling Room in Gloucester Green to use as a café. This also gave a monopoly on catering rights for the area, including a first option on other premises in the vicinity if the Old Settling Room was demolished for any reason. After suitable alterations for its new use it was also opened to the public on the 19th June, along with the SM office noted above. In July the Oxford Corporation deemed Gloucester Green the only officially recognised parking place in the city for passenger vehicles, which was quite a coo indeed in the development of the SM business. The café then became an integral focus of activities at Gloucester Green for passengers and crews alike.

Feeling no doubt he was on a business roll, Beesley decide to apply for a licence variation on the London express to be allowed to pick up and set down in Slough, in those days in the county of Buckinghamshire. The reason for the application was no doubt the realisation that this town was bucking the national trend in isolation therefore undeniably made good business sense. With the country in an ever-deepening depression with almost thirty per cent unemployment, this town seemed immune and could boast continuing growth, plenty of good clean jobs and above average wages. The developing Slough Trading Estate already had the likes of Mars situated in its midst, this Company employing several thousand people assisting in the manufacture of sweets for worldwide distribution.

At Gloucester Green c.1933 is a pair of Scammell & Nephew-bodied 'Tiger' TS3's headed by No.31 (JO 1595), with an Arnold & Comben-bodied Gilford coach in the background. Note the 'Tiger' picture-badge on the radiator top, Leyland scroll and 'By Appointment' badge on the mesh. The oval fleetname panel on the dash, roof-mounted route boards and black-on-white destination blind are other notable period features.

To Beesley's great disappointment the application was refused by the Metropolitan Area Traffic Commissioner, no doubt due in the main to objection by the monopolistic London Passenger Transport Board, which had been created on the first of July in this year, and of course the likes of Thames Valley, Thackray's Way and Red & White, all fearing abstraction.

As a consequence of the outcome of this hearing, meetings took place with the Red & White concern, which in fact controlled all the South Wales booking agents, and an agreement was entered into whereby through ticketing facilities were offered to both companies clientele. This manifested itself whereby an individual could book for instance a journey from Liverpool to Portsmouth, travelling on the R & W express service from Liverpool to Oxford, this ex-Samuelsons service ultimate destination being London, changing at Oxford onto the South Midland Portsmouth-bound coach to continue their journey.

Following on from this, and due in no little part to the pressure being exercised generally by Traffic Commissioners nationwide, pushing for the integration of passenger services to avoid wasteful competition as they saw it, South Midland came to an arrangement next with the then still independent Royal Blue. The agreement encompassed both the SM Oxford - Southsea service and the Royal Blue Birmingham – Coventry – Oxford - Bournemouth route, and mirrored the working arrangement that had been made with the Red & white concern, only in this instance covering passengers from the Midlands who could through book to the Solent and obviously passengers originating in this area who required to travel to the likes of Birmingham, Coventry etc.

On 1st August 1933 the Eastern Counties Omnibus Company Limited, itself a newly formed company out of the origins of four large East Anglian operators, purchased Varsity Express Motors Limited, ostensibly for the Cambridge - London express service, but of course with the take over came the Oxford - London route. Only one noticeable change occurred that of the London final set down and commencement point which now became the Central London Coaching Terminal. South Midland decided at this point for reasons only known to themselves, that the Road Traffic Act was not working out for them, this conclusion being a possible knee-jerk reaction over the result of the Slough pick up application, and that a buyer would be sought for the business.

No buyer was forthcoming in this year although very surprising in several respects. Black & White Motorways had been on the verge of buying the Varsity concern specifically for its Oxford - London service, but felt that the economics of a base in Oxford could only be justified if the SM concern could also be brought under their control, although Varsity had always found the base there an economic proposition. Now, either no approach was made to SM or when an enquiry was made as to if any interest existed for a

58

sale a firm 'no' was received. I would conclude the former suggestion, unbelievable as it might appear, because for South Midland to decide to try and find a buyer for the business would have been the result of several months of discussion at board meetings, so I believe it likely B & W had assumed it stood no chance of winning over SM directors or more likely did not want to compromise the recent relationship that they had fostered with Red & White over the running of express services from South Wales to London.

No vehicles were purchased in this year and given the serious situation the country was in regarding unemployment, many hunger marches now regularly taking place throughout the land, it was not really surprising that the accounts for this year brought to a halt the optimistic mood that had prevailed in previous years reporting, indeed the profits were down and it had been fortunate the outcome had not been worse, with the new working agreements with other concerns playing a large part in SM's survival.

One very interesting event happened at the beginning of the year, and this was the trial in which one of the Gilford coaches was run on creosote. This involved the fitting of what was described as Horne bi-fuel equipment to the Coventry-Climax engine thus enabling the engine to run on this product, a low priced fuel obtained as a by-product of coal, and for the trial period at least the SM coach was dedicated to the Oxford - London service. The device fitted was a combination of a Solex bi-fuel system and a special manifold, which had been designed for use in conjunction with it by J M Horne & Co. Ltd. of 170 Hornsey Road London N6.

During March an engineer from the 'Motor Transport' periodical inspected and rode on the coach, and he reported that it started without the slightest fuss, the amount of exhaust smoke being no greater than normally emitted from a petrol-engined vehicle, and that road acceleration and top gear work was entirely satisfactory. He perceived an odour pervaded the coach, but could not decide if it was objectionable as the only passenger comment he could evoke was ' This is the best disinfected coach I have ridden on'. No peculiarities in the running of the engine such as knocking noises were noticed, but he did state that drawbacks included crank-case dilution, which brings in its train excessive oil consumption, cylinder, piston and bearing wear. To this end it had been decided to run the coach on Wakefield Castolote, which contained a high proportion of the desired grade of plant-derived castor oil. Indeed, it is interesting to note that the use of 'alternative fuels' in by no means a solely modern pre-occupation.

To the specifics of the specialised manifold, he commented that it had been designed with a view to reducing crankcase dilution, while at the same time ensuring the efficient vaporisation of the creosote. In such a matter the operating temperature is obviously of the greatest importance, as if the temperature is too low liquid fuel will find its way into the cylinders, while if it is too high the fuel will form a carbon crust inside the manifold and thus speedily interfere with its efficiency. The chief feature of the manifold, apart from it being a casting combining the induction and exhaust systems, is that large impact surfaces are provided, while a point of difference from similar manifolds is that no external lagging is required to ensure heat retention. Experiments had been carried out with the object of discovering the optimum compression ratio to employ, and it had now been concluded that finality had been reached in that respect, and the South Midland coach was fitted with a cylinder head which gave a compression ratio of 6.5 to 1, as compared with the normal ration of a petrol engine of 4.58 to 1.

Regarding the Solex bi-fuel system, he stated it had been found in the past to be impractical to operate a vehicle entirely on creosote, as under slow-running conditions sufficient heat was not available to ensure the effective vaporisation of the heavy fuel. Accordingly the Solex engineers had decided to use petrol for starting and slow-running purposes and creosote for higher normal operating speeds, therefore the system made use of two carburettors, the main one being a horizontal model minus the slow-running arrangement fitted close to the manifold, and below it the petrol carburettor retaining only its slow-running components. The two carburettors are mechanically linked in such a way that in a closed throttle position, for low speed work, the petrol carburettor supplies fuel, but when the throttle is opened wider the main creosote carburettor comes into operation and the petrol is cut off.

The article finished with some good statistics, fuel consumption on the SM Gilford coach over distances of 240 miles worked out as follows. On bi-fuel 28 gallons of creosote and 3.5 gallons of petrol against 30 gallons of petrol only returned the following respective costs of £1 0s 8.5d against £1 17s 6d, petrol being purchased in nineteen 1933 for 1s 3d a gallon and creosote for 7d a gallon. The outcome of this far reaching experiment are not known, but I think it is safe to assume the technology, as we would term it today, had come too late to have been of general use, being overtaken by the increasingly successful development of the diesel engine. The coach identity has not been recorded, but after the experimental period it reverted to normal petrol operation.

Chapter Ten   To Sell Or Not To Sell

The year 1934 proved no more lucky for South Midland in its search for a buyer, and indeed Beesley and Taylor resigned themselves to the fact this was perhaps no time to be putting out the ' up for sale' sign. Yes, the Road Traffic Act did advance the logic that the business must now have a good deal of worth, and of course it did especially given SM's Oxford location and that city's prominence geographically, historically and with its continuing industrial expansion. Unfortunately no individual, nor even one of the combines for that matter, seemed willing to part with cash in these uncertain times, unless of course the price being asked indicated a quick sale was required due to financial pressures. The latter might indicate to a combine company especially, that here was maybe something for nothing, and probably in negotiation the price could be reduced even further.

Conditions for both operators and passengers alike were very limited at the Lupus Street coach terminal, and led to the decision to construct a purpose built facility to become Victoria Coach Station, opened in March 1932.

South Midland was not in this unenviable position and therefore was never going to find an interest in the business for a decent price. Although no record exists to confirm my opinion, I think it likely Red & White were approached given that a closer relationship with that Company now existed. Indeed, a parallel can be drawn with the events recorded in Paul Lacey's book *'Thackrays Way – A Family In Road Transport'* (which is in itself a highly recommended read), when this thriving Company officially known as the Ledbury Transport Company Limited, held talks with R & W. The runaway success of the business, together with its strategic position at the meeting of the London, Oxford and Bath roads, led Robert Thackray to decide upon an asking price of £65,000. Although that was quite justifiable in that year for the business, Red & White very politely declined, regarding the asking price as far too high for the prevailing times. However, as Tillings were to pay £68,000 for the business only two years later, it appears that the business had been very competitively priced previously.

Another reason that undoubtedly proved something of a nuisance to SM was its very position as an independent not really treading on anyone's toes, whilst co-operating extensively with large operators. So, any one Company purchasing South Midland at this present point in time could be accused of upsetting the status quo, as formal (or even sometimes informal) agreements now having become *de rigueur* within the industry. Following on from a non-sale of the Company it was decided that SM would be run directly by William Beesley and William Ling Taylor, without regular consultation and debate with other shareholders. I don't detect here any great falling out amongst the board members, rather more an official recognition that William Beesley was the 'hands on' guy on a daily basis, who had now proved himself an astute businessman. His decisions could be respected and were usually totally supported, the fact that he may have run matters through Taylor was only to be expected as he still was SM's main backer, although I doubt he ever disagreed with Beesley, his protégé, who had proved himself many times over.

William Taylor had in fact become godfather the year previous to Beesley's only son Christopher, his other three children all being girls, Pat born in 1924 (my reference point incidentally), Daphne born 1931 and later on in 1936 another daughter Shirley would be born. William Taylor had never given up his full time senior position with the Forestry Commission, so again it made good business sense to rely on the man who best new the business inside out and was instrumental in its achieving a dominant position in the Oxford express coach market.

On Sunday 22nd April 1934 Varsity was placed under the wing of United Counties, and as this Company's head office was in Northampton it was slightly better placed than Eastern Counties to manage the business (both being Tilling Group members). However, I have never understood why the

Thames Valley Traction Company (in which Tilling was a substantial shareholder at this juncture) was not chosen to control the business from Reading. As it also had a base at High Wycombe through which the Varsity express to London operated, the maintenance and garaging aspects would have made sense. But I digress, as that didn't happen, and UC continued to operate Varsity more as a temporary subsidiary up until Monday 9th July in this year, when the final set down point in London and correspondingly the London departure point became Victoria Coach Station, but more on this later.

May saw the delivery of the only vehicle to be ordered for this year, again a Leyland 'Tiger', though this time a TS6 model, which like the TS4 delivered two years previously would remain 'one of a kind' within the fleet. Harrington again supplied the body, a 32-seater front-entrance type, and this became No.33 (AFC 531). Although no firm date is to hand, it is probable that the first of the Lancias (WL 2696) was sold about that time.

Bearing classic split-level waistrail Harrington coachwork, the TS6 was a fine looking coach. It was caught by the camera on a layover at Southsea.

On 1st July Associated Motorways was formed, and as much has already been written regarding that organisation, suffice it to say here that it was a formation essentially born out of falling passenger numbers, unwanted competition and the desire of the Traffic Commissioners to see express operators work more co-operatively. It was an immediate success, with its member companies initially comprising Midland Red (BMMO), Black &

White Motorways, Royal Blue (Elliott Bros.), Greyhound Motors Ltd., Red & White Services Ltd and United Counties Omnibus Co. Ltd. Between them they covered some four and three quarter million miles of express operation, so it could never have been anything else but just that.

The relevance to South Midland of this organisation, although they probably were completely unaware of it at the time, was a stipulation that United Counties had insisted on being inserted into the Agreement, and which no other member sought to mirror for there respective operating territories. It was unique and read as follows verbatim:- *'That in the event of any of the Companies acquiring any such service as falls within the provisions of this clause the Company shall forthwith upon the acquisition of such service notify the Committee of such acquisition and the terms of it as to price or otherwise, and offer same to the Committee at same price, and unless within one month from the date of such notification and offer the Committee shall on behalf of the said Companies agree to acquire such service from the Company concerned at the price at and on the terms on which the same was acquired or at such other lesser price or on such other terms as may be agreed the Company acquiring that service shall be at liberty to operate the same free from the restrictions in this clause contained. Provided that this paragraph shall not apply to the acquisition by the United Counties Omnibus Co Ltd., of the South Midland services between Oxford and London'.*

From this paragraph one can assume Mr Beesley's wish to sell SM had not fallen completely on deaf ears. United Counties had perhaps believed the Company was doomed financially, but certainly it had designs on South Midland, and no doubt in the event of succeeding it would have given the Worcester-Oxford-Southsea express over to Associated Motorways, as it had specifically excluding this service from the inserted line of the Agreement, which I guess would have been operated by Midland Red.

Locally in Oxford, the Varsity advertisements in the newspapers became larger, proclaiming the Company was now booking agents for Crosville Motor Services and emphasising that the business was now ' United Counties in association with Varsity', but that Company's biggest announcement and advertisement came at the beginning of July when it informed the public that a new timetable was to commence on Monday July 9th 1934 to London Victoria as follows, Monday-Saturday daily ex-Oxford 08.00am, 09.35am, 10.45am, 01.35pm, 03.00pm, 4.35pm, 6.15pm and 08.00pm. Ex-London weekdays 06.30am (Mons. only), 09.15am, 10.45am,

Side by side at Gloucester Green in 1935 are brand new blue-liveried United Counties Leyland 'Tiger' TS7 with Eastern Counties body No.405 (VV 3775), and South Midland 'Tiger' TS3 No.31 (JO 1595), still with its original Scammell & Nepthew body.

12.45pm, 02.30pm, 04.45pm, 06.30pm, 08.30pm and 11.45pm. Eight journeys daily (one more than South Midland), the early morning Monday departure being dropped less than a year later, the Sunday services consisting of six journeys in each direction, (again one extra than SM), and the Sunday times as follows ex-Oxford 08.15am, 10.00am, 02.35pm, 06.15pm, 08.00pm and 09.15pm and ex-London 09.45am, 10.45am, 02.30pm, 06.30pm, 09.00pm and 10.45pm.

At last SM managed to find a vehicle for a little excursion work, as in August this year every Thursday and Sunday departing at 07.30am a trip was advertised to Bournemouth. The dramatic reduction in excursion work was no doubt due to the competition being experienced all through the summer season from the railways who had implemented huge fare reductions, which impacted on SM's turnover and consequently profits.

The news at the beginning of 1935, no doubt surprised many, was that yet another independent operator had been purchased by a combine. This however no ordinary independent, but the famous Bournemouth-based Royal Blue, the Elliott family deciding to sell to Tilling's, all the more remarkable as Royal Blue was well established had expanded considerably and had been instrumental in the formation of Associated Motorways in

65

'thirty four. From the South Midland perspective, it must have felt very vulnerable, with United Counties now in control of Varsity and as an AM member likely to get the lions share of through bookings. I suspect that even COMS might have had a little shudder as a result, feeling a degree of abstraction regarding bookings might now happen, passengers likely to use the Varsity office for long distance bookings. This was not welcome news, coming at a time when South Midland was struggling to balance the books and needed urgently to reverse this continuing trend.

Although the two mechanics SM had at this time, long serving employees Mr Bessell and Mr Filer were dedicated individuals who had between them kept the fleet on the road under very difficult operating conditions, they were now battling with some time expired equipment. The Lancia's and Dennis models from the mid to late 1920's had high mileage, though having given sterling service, and were now beginning to cost money. Beesley decided on a clear out of the older or less efficient units as circumstances permitted through 1935. In January Gilford No.24 (WL 9810) was disposed off, followed by No.27 (JO 200) in February, and another Gilford No.23 (WL 9415) in March. May saw the sale of Lancia WL 4131, followed by the other of that type, No.14 (WL 5055) in June.

By now a loyal Leyland customer, South Midland would be on the New Year calendar list of Leyland Motors, and did in actual fact receive calendars annually from this year on, William Beesley's daughter recalling what splendid works of art they were proudly proclaiming ' The Leyland She's a Lady'. With the arrival in the fleet of the first of the Leyland 'Tiger' TS7's in time for the season start in April, as No.34 (BFC 675) with Harrington 32-seat front entrance body. This was followed in May by No.35 (BWL 349) with Harrington 32-seat rear entrance body, and they heralded a new optimism, with oil engined vehicles reducing operating costs, which along with the fleet reduction from twenty one vehicles down to eighteen saw no decline in efficiency levels.

Also about this time a secondhand 20-seater coach was purchased, perhaps to perpetuate the need to have a smaller vehicle for private hire work. This vehicle is, however, not well documented, though it appears to have been owned from about the Summer of 1935 until disposed off by March 1941. It was a normal-control Morris Commercial 'Viceroy', new in July 1931 and bearing registration number HA 7493. It has been suggested that it was originally a demonstration vehicle for Morris Commercial, which would certainly account for the Birmingham mark. However, despite research on a wide front, no firm details are known of its early history. It certainly appeared on an insurance schedule of coaches owned by SM in May 1937, but to date no photographs of it have come to light, so the make of body is also unknown. It has been recorded elsewhere that this coach carried fleet number 33, though that was not actually vacated until 1940, but in view of disposals around the time of its arrival No.23 would seem a possibility.

Although no photos of HA 7493 are known, this 'Viceroy' was actually the previous chassis off the Morris Commercial production line and serves to illustrate the front end appearance of the model. It was one of a pair new to Isle of Wight operator Walkden's Bus Service of Sandown.

With fares to London now 4/9d single, 6/- day return and 8/6d period return traffic was very slowly increasing, and in addition a more concerted effort was being made to increase private hire traffic once again, this having been South Midlands' 'roots'. During the summer various excursions were advertised, in the June for instance a coach was advertised to run every single day of the seven day Aldershot Military Tattoo departing Oxford at 06.00pm, Ascot Races a four day gala event again a coach was advertised for each day departing 09.00am, whilst the Royal Air Force Pageant at

67

Hendon on 29th June in this year was another venue SM would run a coach to. In that month also SM were going all out to promote the Crosville-operated Chester - Birkenhead - Liverpool service for 22/6d, which I guess followed approaches from Crosville management, who were possibly concerned at the lack of interest now being shown by United Counties, the resulting change being one up to South Midland!

In July a particularly popular event was the four day Silver Jubilee Naval Review at Portsmouth from the 13th – 16th inclusive, to which SM ran coaches daily. On the last day the vehicles did not leave Portsmouth until very late, so that everyone who had been conveyed that day could see the farewell illuminations, which was a nice touch. August saw more daily excursions but these were the usual repeats of past years Stratford-upon-Avon, Whipsnade Zoo, the Berkshire Downs and a tour of Bibury, though they must have still been very popular. Tidworth Military Tattoo was considered by many, including my dear departed mum who regularly saw both the Aldershot and Tidworth events, to be superior to the Aldershot display was advertised by both South Midland and Varsity, so this maybe proved the point conclusively.

Driver H. E. Surman, one of the two brothers who were South Midland's original drivers, contributed to the good reputation for courtesy and safety.

With the end of the Summer season, it was decided to dispose of a further Gilford, this time No.25 (WL 9862), which was sold in October. It is worth noting that the pair of Dennis F-types, built in 1929, remained in service despite the withdrawal of newer vehicles, no doubt much to their credit.

Chapter Eleven   Sussex By The Sea

At the South Midland Board Meeting on 22nd October 1935 a suggestion was made that a hire car business might be considered either at Brighton or some such town.

At the following meeting on 15th November it was resolved that Brighton would be the chosen town. The large Jubilee Street garage of George Newman & Co. (Brighton) Ltd. was available at that time, though at 118 cars the capacity was much higher than required. It was resolved to make an offer for the garage and to consider ordering 20 Vauxhall 12hp Light Six cars. In consideration, the additional garage space could be rented out to offset the costs of the new venture, though it was anticipated that this arrangement would only last until a purpose-built garage could be provided.

Subsequently the Jubilee Road premises were not secured, so a collection of lock-up units at St. James Street Mews, off Cavendish Road and close to the Old Steine and sea-front areas, was acquired on lease early in February 1936. The new venture was to be called *Britax*, the inspiration apparently having come from the title *Citax* used by a similar concern in the City of Oxford.

The original choice of vehicle type was soon changed to the Austin 'Ascot' 12hp, 10 of which would be standard saloon bodies, whilst the other half of the order would have sun-saloon roofs, a feature likely to make them rather attractive for Summer use. The bodywork featured a glazed screen separating the driver from the 4 passengers, who sat in pairs facing each other.

Operation commenced on Saturday 14th March 1936, and the accompanying advertisement in the 'Brighton Herald' fully informed the public of this new facility. The service would operate only as a private hire, with no cars featuring on the town's cab ranks, but would have the added advantage of being available 24 hours a day. A rate of 8 old pence for the first mile, followed by a further 2 d for each additional quarter mile represented a very good rate for that class of work. The same rate would apply for any hour or day of the week, and fares only commenced from the pick-up point. It was further stated that, although the service was regarded as a local operation, longer distance hires were also possible.

The operation obviously favoured the more well-off clientelle, or at least those with access to a telephone, as all bookings were based on that facility. To identify the cars the legend *BRITAX* was carried on the bonnet sides, with the lettering painted onto a lighter background outline of an arrow shape. The car used in the inaugural advert was CCD 791, but fuller details of the fleet are lacking.

The service got off to a very good start, and before the end of March the rent of a yard at 35 Raphael Road in Hove had been added to reduce dead mileage on operations in that direction. The location was conveniently situated between the Hove and Dyke Halt stations and the sea-front at the Western Esplanade.

A 1936 Austin 'Ascot' of the type used for the 'Britax' venture

Such was the success of the venture that a further 10 Austins were ordered in July 1936, followed by 6 more by the end of November that year. By that point in time the cars had run 329,700 miles and carried 122,227 miles, showing that most journeys were indeed of a local nature. It should of course be appreciated that not only was car ownership quite low then, it was also relatively difficult to keep a car on the road throughout the rigours of the British Winter in those days. Added to that a sizeable number of residents who habitually lived in hotels, together with numerous regular visitors who could afford such transport, and the choice of Brighton was soon vindicated.

However, after a certain point of expansion, the demand seems to have reached its maximum some way short of the earlier indications. The failure to reach expectations was largely blamed on the inefficiency of the local phone system, resulting in some of the cars being disposed of by December 1937. Despite that setback there were 138,383 jobs, 634,665 miles and 258,058 passengers carried that year.

Parking in Hove was altered during September to some lock-up garages, though the exact location has not been recorded.

By the close of the following year *Britax* had actually lost £100, though this was not considered too serious, as it was resolvable by further reducing the number of cars yet again. However, despite the foregoing, the Board actually considered a proposal to start a similar venture in Coventry at the April 1939 meeting. Nothing more of this is heard of with *South Midland*, though it is understood that Beesley did invest in his own right in such an operation in Cheltenham under the name *Cheltax*.

In the meantime *Britax* had continued with 30 cars, when further consideration was given to the operations there in December 1939. It was appreciated that replacements vehicles would become difficult to obtain, whilst the value of the cars would begin to rise now that peacetime production ceased. Operation continued, though by January 1940 the service was suffering from petrol rationing and a 25% increase in fares.

Further fuel restrictions led to the operation ceasing from 1st August 1942, though the business was not closed down until mid December. During that time the cars were overhauled prior to sale, with 15 having been disposed of at a profit by the end of the year. Surplus garage space was rented out until the lease was finally surrendered in March 1943. And so the Brighton business, and indeed the Company's involvement with taxis was discontinued. It is, of course, interesting to speculate that if the operation had survived until the sale to *Red & White*, then it might have been revived once the war had ended.

Above – this advert block from the 1936 Oxford Guide summarises the SM position at this point. The early years of hard work had established it as an operator with well-maintained coaches, courteous drivers and soundly organised. Membership of London Coastal Coaches, unusual for a small independent operator had also been a good investment. Below – One of the 1936 Harrington-bodied Leyland 'Tiger' TS7's at Victoria Coach Station.

Chapter Twelve   Storm Clouds

Very pleased with the Leyland TS7's, SM ordered two more this time both front entrance 32-seaters for delivery April 1936, the Company finding that despite initial outlay the diesel engined-'Tigers' were proving a winner both with customers, drivers and the accountants alike. The tide had been turned by mid year by the actions taken, boosting the accounts to a satisfactory level, the main savings stemming from a large reduction in maintenance costs. The effort put into reviving the private hire business had been a resounding success, and passenger numbers had also increased slightly on the express services. The only disappointing news was that the café in Gloucester Green, which as mentioned had a monopoly in the immediate area of the Green, had only a very poor level of income.

The theme of reducing operating costs continued throughout 1936, attention turning to the 5-year old Leyland 'Tiger' TS3, which had proven very reliable chassis. However, the same could not be said regarding the Scammell & Nephew bodies, whose deterioration was now the cause of some concern. So William Beesley decided to rebody them, the order for the work going to his friend Harrington. They were taken to Hove to have 28-seat front entrance coach bodies fitted for a price of £585 each, which effectively made them look to the public, at least, like brand new coaches.

TS3 'Tiger' No.29 (JO 1599) after re-bodying with its new Harrington body, smartly turned out in red and cream 'streamlined' livery of the day. These were fitted with sliding roofs and a neat front destination layout.

The two completely new coaches arrived in the April as promised, as Nos. 36 and 37 (CWL 951 and 953), also sporting Harrington coachwork on TS7 chassis. The year for all intense and purpose mirrored the previous year in the majority of areas, fairly unexciting but very positive, the boardroom now very much into the new hire car business. However, there was one big improvement and that was the café which increased takings by over 300% and made a healthy profit. In fact the Company's optimism was such that it believed all the changes it had made were working and to quote 'the decline had been halted'.

'Tiger' TS7 No.36 (CWL 951) photographed when new for contemporary Harrington publicity. The cream area above the side windows was fitted with route boards, whilst the interiors were amongst the best on offer.

Following delivery of the additional TS7's, another Gilford was released, with No.21 (WL 9079) departing during June 1936.

1936 had seen an increase in express passenger numbers in the Country generally for some reason, slowly but surely, but 1937 saw an explosion in the numbers travelling in this way. South Midland were no exception to this unexpected boom, and in fact it would turn out to be the best year in SM's history to date, with 3500 more passengers than in 1936 on express services alone, equivalent to 120 extra coaches. Whilst obviously some spare capacity had existed, it is quite clear many extra coach loads had to be catered for, much of the traffic to London, itself now becoming ever popular, with many passengers using the connecting services from Victoria to reach the east and south-east coastal resorts.

Whether by accident or design, given the brisk business now being enjoyed, SM chose to change the outside cover of the Company timetables and advertisement headings at this time. Both now adorned by what appeared to be a driver or inspector wearing a peak cap and speaking through a very large loudspeaker declaring *'all aboard'*, although sounding basic by today's standards, the effect was very modern in appearance for the time. Much of the South Midland promotional material was given over to the impending Coronation and was advertised thus *'London's Gay come and enjoy yourself'*, need I say more, don't times change. No vehicles had been ordered for this year, as fleet consolidation had been completed and productivity levels maintained.

The lease on 111 St Aldates was due to run out in March 1938, and notice had been duly received to quit. Fortunately South Midland had been able to purchase a lease for 118 High Street, Oxford, just down the road from the COMS office, so as the time arrived the business was able to continue uninterrupted. With 'thirty seven finishing on a high, it was even more surprising to see this trend not only continue into 1938, but significantly more business come SM's way. It was as if the Nation at least, if not Neville Chamberlain's appeasement Government of the day, believed a war with Germany inevitable and was making hay while the sun shone. The unemployment situation was also easing as production started on the likes of ships, aircraft and armaments, if a little late in the day, with Hitler's troops now in Austria and shortly to enter Czechoslovakia.

By the year end an additional 7000 passengers over 1937 would travel on SM's express services, equating to well over 200 extra coaches, and in all probability this number of extra coaches in this year was required, the uptake of the previous two years now having filled vehicles to capacity. In complete contrast to the increasing passenger numbers being experienced, South Midland in the February and March of this year took delivery, one in each month, of two small capacity Leyland 'Cub' SKPZ2-types. There was evidently a requirement for 26-seaters, as these were replacements for the pair of Dennis F-types, Nos.16 and 17 (WL 7240 and 7256), both of which were disposed of in May 1937. Front entrance Harrington coach bodies were fitted to the newcomers, which were Nos. 24 and 25 (FWL 795/7). The use of non-sequential registration numbers is once again evident.

United Counties belatedly caught up with the large SM advert campaign, which to a degree may have been part of the success story in attracting extra passengers, and in June similarly produced such promotional material

The forward-control Leyland 'Cub' was fairly rare, and SM's examples carried a scaled-down version of the Harrington body of the time. These were useful coaches for smaller hire parties but, like all members of the fleet, were also used on the express workings. No.24 (FWL 795) is seen at Victoria Coach Station during 1938.

for the London express service, though it was actually of a slightly larger size - a case of anything SM can do, UC can do better! The advertisements depicted a coach with the slogan *'Ride the highways see the byways by coach enjoy the journey by travelling the United Counties way'*, but note the Varsity connection is no longer mentioned. Within a week SM had reacted by placing advertisements of the same size, now illustrating a London skyline of that City's most famous buildings in black print, with a white coach, not any recognisable chassis or body make, set against this background. It looked very professional, and rumour has it that Beesley designed it himself.

Ironically, just as the Company was enjoying several very good years in a row from a trading perspective, which would normally signal a rosy future, the future itself was far from such. With Europe now beginning to be dominated by Hitler's Nazi Germany, it was clear that many things would change radically, and not I fear for the better. Although many saw a further war as probably inevitable, few could appreciate how long such a conflict and its aftermath might last, nor indeed the devastating effect on daily life.

76

Chapter Thirteen   War and Peace

And so into 1939, which would be the last 'normal' year for a while to come. Business was still very brisk, as optimism was rife at least in the business sense, and indeed many people held the firm belief that war was not inevitable, many taking the attitude Europe's problems were just that, Europe's problems. Although we all know hindsight is a wonderful thing, it still defies belief that anyone could have been so naïve as to believe that ultimately, even if this country had not been attacked until all of Europe was under Hitler's control, he would not have left this island alone. If that scenario had been played out, of course we all know this island would have been overrun within days at that point, no if's or but's.

The new SM headquarters and booking office at 118 High Street, Oxford.

However back to the South Midland story at this point in time, January opened the year with surprisingly the same large type of advertisement being displayed in the local newspapers as used during the season in 1938. This was unusual as in previous years, quite understandably, the first few quiet months up to March would have seen very little advertising, if at all.

It was probably considered a waste of money and effort, as travel into the new year was very limited, almost only if essential, but obviously now thought very necessary by SM to keep the momentum of increasing ridership going. United Counties reverted to a very small advert, however the probable reason was that City of Oxford Motor Services was now boldly proclaiming that their office at 138 High Street Oxford was the place to book for the London express of United Counties.

Quite strange would be the best description of this arrangement. Yes, United Counties was a member of Associated Motorways, and COMS by virtue of its twenty per cent holding in Black & White were part of the 'club', but the London service was not part of AM. UC was of course a Tilling company, and COMS was a BET member, whilst B&W had a regular headway from Gloucester / Cheltenham to London, so I would have thought COMS priority would have been to promote that service. Both SM and UC continued with the modern styling of advertisements in the press as used in 'thirty-eight.

William Beesley decided on a policy change for vehicle specification in this year, buoyed up by the phenomenal passenger increases taking place, he had ordered four chassis for this year, two which would be delivered on time as usual ready for the season start in March, these being of the Leyland 'Cheetah' model. Several of the large Leyland users such as Southdown and Ribble had also taken this type into stock instead of the ubiquitous 'Tiger' chassis. The merits of the model was that it was over a ton lighter in weight compared to the 'Tiger', was recommended by Leyland as a short to medium distance vehicle when used in coaching form, and the noise reduction, when specified with a petrol engine, was allegedly 'unbelievable, the vehicle seemingly to whistle along'. With such a description, and given the sixty miles or thereabouts to London from Oxford, a route most SM vehicles spent their time on, especially in the first few years after being placed in service, it is perhaps understandable why Beesley reverted to petrol, but I suggest customer attraction had been paramount in his mind, as the diesel engine had played more than a passing part in the rejuvenation of SM when it was going through a bad patch.

On delivery, very surprisingly, they would be found to have been bodied by Burlingham, William Beesley appearing to have deserted his old friend Harrington. The likely reason however was that with many passenger transport companies finding a new confidence, and all enjoying increasing patronage, Harrington may well have been unable to facilitate the delivery dates required by SM, although on the other side of the coin, it could be argued as a friend he would have ensured delivery as requested by Beesley, so on balance perhaps it was decided to change the bodybuilder just to compare the two manufacturers products? 32-seat front entrance coach bodies were fitted to these vehicles, fleet numbers 26 and 27 (HFC548 and HFC 550).

Leyland 'Cheetah' No.27 (HFC 550) seen at Newbury Wharf later in its life. These coaches worked hard throughout the war years, hence the lack of an offside headlamp? This early post-war view also celebrates the return of the popular Southsea route.

It was Burlingham who also bodied the third coach to arrive in the August, fleet No.23 (JFC 12), again reverting to available numbers previously used, in this instance originally a Gilford 168OT, and also possibly used for the Morris Commercial 'Viceroy'. This practice was slightly ironic, given Beesley in the earlier years had commenced fleet identification at a high number, clearly to give the impression of a larger fleet than was actually the case, one would therefore have expected the numbers to have continued in sequence to that last used!

Vehicles departing the fleet during 1939 were Gilford 168OT's Nos.22 and 26 (WL 9081 and 9942), which were sold in June and May respectively. The 20-seat 'Viceroy' (HA 7493) also left early in the war, though no firm

79

The first Austin was also amongst the first of that type built. No.23 (JFC 12), could be considered as that maker's alternative to the Bedford WTB of the immediate pre-war period.

date has been ascertained, partly because it could still be seen around with its new owners House Bros. of Watlington.

This third vehicle again sprung a surprise, in that it was an Austin K3 with 26-seat front entrance body, again petrol engined, very much a lightweight chassis. Mass produced, and under normal circumstances would not be considered a long life vehicle - though the initial price was certainly lower than a 'Cheetah', Beesley evidently experimenting with a view on how to go forward fleet wise. Also delivered in August was Austin K3, fleet No.22 (JFC 42), but this time with a Harrington 26-seat front entrance body. This particular vehicle continued the SM surprises of this year, and visually was the biggest one, as it was delivered in a livery of red and yellow. This fact was authenticated not only by the registering of the vehicle, but William Beesley's daughter remembers a red and yellow coach, this being mentioned by her to me before I had seen the registration document. I also received a letter during compiling this history, from transport historian John Gillham, who lives in West London, and in it he stated remembering a SM coach during this period ' being painted bright yellow, with bright red wings and I believe a bright red roof'.

It was probably an idea born out of trying to project the Company image more universally, and fix the name of South Midland in people's minds, if for no other reason than by virtue of the fact the livery might well become a talking point. This would promote the Company further by associating the colour scheme/name to become synonymous with travel to and from London, and more locally when organisations and businesses were considering hiring a coach. It was not however a policy furthered by SM and no other vehicles were delivered or repainted in this scheme, red and cream remaining the South Midland colours.

In April United Counties tinkered with the Monday-Saturday departure times of the Oxford-London express service, but nothing of real significance emerged other than an announcement at the same time that as from the first Monday in May until the last Monday in September, and on Mondays only, from London a 06.30am service to Oxford would operate - a real case of *deja vu*. Over the summer months South Midland introduced a regular selected day and half day tours programme, a revival of something tried in years past, this time around Monday, Wednesday and Friday saw day excursions to Stratford-on-Avon and Cheddar Caves, and half day to Bibury and Cirencester and a separate tour to Burnham Beeches near Slough. Tuesday, Thursday and Sunday day excursions to Bournemouth and a Tour of the Wye Valley and half day to Whipsnade Zoo and Bourton-on-the-Water.

A popular pre-war destination was the inland 'resort' near Wokingham known as 'California-in-England', where 'Tiger' No.29 (JO 1599) is seen.

During August Emergency Regulations were brought into being by the Government of the day, in the light of the deepening crisis now so obviously emerging in Europe. Regulation 104 had a section dealing with public safety, providing for compulsory evacuation of people by order of the Secretary of State, also including powers to control rail and road traffic. On the 1st September 1939 Hitler marched into Poland, having seized Czechoslavakia in the Spring which had broken the Munich Agreement, Chamberlain at last waking up to the fact the Dictator could not be trusted. On the 3rd September, Britain and France declared war on Germany.

A few days before on the 31st August, the compulsory order had been given using Regulation 104 referred to, to transport three million people from cities and towns throughout the country, the great majority school children. It is not specifically known what input South Midland had in this process, and certainly large numbers travelled by train from the cities, although later moved by bus and coach from the stations they arrived at. Logically where South Midland may have assisted would have been in that the authorities likely utilised the express timings from London's Victoria Coach Station, plus additional vehicles as required, the express services running in any case as timetabled, this also helping to stagger the mass exodus, which lasted from the 1st - 4th September.

Even after this immediate period traffic would continue to be extremely heavy due to the many adults leaving during the following months, although many people remained in London. In November the Company was instructed to reduce mileage to save fuel, the casualties were the 07.15am and 12.30pm departures ex-Oxford and the 03.00pm and 09.00pm timings ex-London. To end this rather overshadowed year William Beesley met William Taylor to discuss the situation on the 3rd December at the White Hart public house at Tetbury, where it was agreed to reserve two new chassis for the future, a very optimistic view given the state of things. It was also decided that whilst the hostilities ensued the White Hart would, until further notice, become the regular meeting place, a sort of safe house it was hoped, and in any event approximately half way between Oxford and the Forest of Dean, the homes respectively of the owners of South Midland.

With the arrival of 1940, transport matters were now controlled by what was referred to as Regional Traffic Commissioners, the individual responsible for the Oxford area being based in Reading, not too popular locally given the location in a different county. Amongst the RTC duties, he could direct where vehicles were allocated and drivers worked. In

82

February the War Department requisitioned Gilford No.20 (WL 9076) for duties as required, and shortly after that No.33 (AFC 531), the solitary SM Leyland 'Tiger' TS6. One would assume Beesley had no choice which chassis were removed, though the military particularly liked coaches with sliding roofs for the ease of mounting of bren guns. Three further coaches were converted to ambulances, using kits provided for this purpose, should they be required in an emergency, though they doubtless reverted to normal seating in due course. Gilford No.19 (WL 9058) was involved in conversion, but the identity of the other examples is not known. However, SM's involvement in an ambulance service would take a new serious twist very soon.

Another view of the first Austin No.23 (JFC 12) shows the streamlined style of the period. On the glass rain-shields over the side windows can be seen the place names London – Henley – Oxford – Worcester in gold lettering.

A new vehicle, another Austin K3 with Harrington twenty six seat front entrance coach body arrived in either March or April, becoming No.21 (JFC 707). South Midland was very fortunate to receive this vehicle under the circumstances, but it would perhaps lift morale a little for passengers lucky enough to travel on such a new vehicle. This period in 1940 was known as the 'phoney war', but Britain's inhabitants were soon confronted with the real thing. The British Expeditionary Force that had been sent to France, with the aim of intercepting the German Army, received a 'pounding' and were required to withdraw, resulting over the period May to June in the deaths of some half a million British military personnel. In spite of this terrible tragedy a miracle did occur, in that around 300,000 servicemen were eventually evacuated back to these shores. This is often portrayed as an armada of small boats ferrying the soldiers home, the feat accomplished in a few days. The fact that ordinary folk took their boats to France in very dangerous conditions to save British lives was true, though the miracle however was that they repeated this trip over and over again for up to two months, if they were lucky enough to survive without getting blown up or shot, as it took all of May and June of this year to complete the evacuation. It was truly a miracle of miracles was that anyone was left alive after a week, let alone months, to bring home.

South Midland very much came into the picture as events unfolded, and Pat Beesley remembers vividly in the first few weeks of the evacuation SM coaches bringing to Oxford the injured, although from what location they had landed she has no idea. Again, it is often portrayed as if Dover was the only arrival point, when in reality all along the south coast boats landed, often at the boat owners home port, so it is likely South Midland vehicles had gone to Southampton. I was also left with the impression that at certain times many coaches of SM would be used at one time, the majority, maybe through urgency, not converted to ambulance format to ferry the injured. William Beesley personally oversaw the arrival back of his coaches from such trips, often advising many of the well-wishers that greeted back the soldiers, not to stare too intently at the 'boys', given their horrendous ordeal and the often obvious serious injuries.

No sooner had the last of the soldiers managed to get back, than the country was faced with the infamous 'Battle of Britain', which commenced around the 10th July. This consisted mainly of attacking airfields, and with the small force of aircraft in service, the country witnessed its second miracle when, over a period of 3 months of almost daily attacks. The Royal Air Force triumphed over the Luftwaffe and again the Country lived to fight another day, Surprisingly, considering the numbers of airfields surrounding Oxford, the papers of the day reported little in the way of enemy attack, seemingly more aircraft crashes stemming from RAF flying accidents, and this was confirmed by research of documents published post war on such matters.

South Midland were still running the five departures daily from both Oxford and London, with only one service in each direction now to Worcester, requiring the driver to night out in London. Board was usually found at 'The Greyhound' public house, which since the 'thirties had been used by South Midland crews and many other coach drivers as well who frequented Victoria Coach Station - and remained so for SM drivers whilst

84

At this point in the war no-one could have foreseen quite how long it would be before carefree scenes such as this outing to horse-racing could return. Re-bodied 'Tiger' TS3 No.30 (JO 1593) prepares to leave the Gloucester Green café accompanied by 'Cheetah' No.27 (HFC 550).

the London express service was operating up until at least the early 'fifties. It was located in Cambridge Street SW1, a short distance from the coach station. United Counties were advertising in July for the London express, on the basis of 'A seat assured', though one wonders in these times why advertising would be necessary. One further has to call into question how in wartime any seat could be assured, when at short notice the RTC could direct the vehicles to where he so deemed, a mystery that one and a possible waste of money.

The next phase in Hitler's grand plan would have catastrophic results, this being the commencement of daily bombing raids on London, eventually to encapsulate many industrial areas of the country, but initially on the Capital. Starting with a few daytime raids in the August of this year, but to

85

become soon nightly raids from September, and in that month alone 5,300 tons of explosives dropped on London in just twenty four nights, with anything from 200-400 aircraft each night. Much has been written about the heroism of coach drivers during the 'Blitz', but when put into perspective that in addition to taking a chance on being bombed, drivers had the added problem of masked headlights when driving and in bad weather, a winter 'smog' being usual in London, and with visibility nil effectively, the task they faced was enormous.

When describing these conditions the name of Ted Surman raises its head again, this original driver of William Beesley's South Midland, renowned for his ability to manoeuvre his coach through London like no other. Another driver who worked for SM then recalled to me one such journey, when he had no idea on leaving Victoria Coach Station at night where he was, as he could hardly see his hand in front of him. He concluded they would not be able to embark on the route to Oxford that night, but he was driving a relief coach to Ted's scheduled vehicle, and the latter was certainly not about to let his passengers down. So, on departing he virtually attached his coach to Ted's, so close as to be able to see the tail lights, to this day he has no idea how Ted navigated himself to Oxford, no obstacles were hit, not even an occasional kerb, and he mused that after that journey he believed Ted could have driven the route daily blindfolded, such was his knowledge of that road. As a postscript several passengers in his coach later sent letters into Beesley praising his driving that night, but not one single passenger on Ted's coach had written in a similar gesture! Throughout early 1940 the Government had taken measures to move all Departments out of London to so called 'safe areas', this involving various transport companies including South Midland, who for whatever reason seemed to be allocated by the Regional Traffic Commissioner work emanating from the London area. Finally, and ironic as it may seem, SM in the April and May had operated excursions to Southsea and a Tour of Bibury and Bourton-on-the-Water, with COMS also receiving authority at this time to operate to Whipsnade Zoo and a tour of the Berkshire Downs, the last such luxuries for the public for a number of years.

1941 saw the 'Blitz' of London continue, and many other centres of population throughout the Country were now receiving 'hits', although thankfully by the May these had begun to diminish and into the summer quite considerably. However although initially some 15% of the Capital's population had left by the end of 1939, during the early part of the following year a great number had returned, deciding it was a lot of fuss about nothing. The bombing of London had changed all that again, large numbers leaving by any means possible. One of the drivers of South Midland at the time, regrettably no longer with us today, Tom Lynch, would often come back home to his family with sad stories of what he had witnessed on his trips, his daughter Winifred kind enough to write to me with some brief details. Tom had been a driver with South Midland since about 1932 and Win, as she prefers to be called, travelled pre-war many times on her dad's coach. She well remembers the brown and gold rugs supplied by SM to passengers to keep them warm in the winter time, which by all accounts were very effective, such was the quality.

She also remembers distinctly her father bringing coach loads of evacuees back to Oxford, but believes they were as a result of people being bombed out, not a government backed evacuation as in the early war years, because depending on the previous night's devastation, it would effect the number of people found waiting for his coach on arrival at the terminal, in fact waiting for any coach from almost anywhere to arrive. On one occasion on arrival at Victoria Tom found Win's grandparents just sitting there at the coach station, their home apparently a heap of rubble, so needless to say Tom brought them back to Oxford where they stayed for the duration. On another trip he arrived to find among many that morning a cousin who told a similar story to the grandparents, again Tom offered his home.

But of course the same sad traumatic story applied to hundreds, quite what many of them did on arrival at the various destinations if they had no family or connections, and many in desperation took the route of jumping on the first available coach to leave London, would be uncertain, possibly the Salvation Army assisted where possible. Another sad story recalled was of a young girl who was found by Tom at Victoria with nothing but the clothes she wore and an extremely heavy Singer sewing machine, which she could barely lift, all that she had managed to salvage, each of these stories illustrating the sad real truth of war.

South Midland had been engaged, possibly along with other operators, because of continuing bombing to move BBC personnel to other locations in the country One specific job SM had been tasked with in this connection, was to bring the news team to Oxford, it is believed to Blenheim Palace, and Win remembers her father referring to Alvar Le Dell, a well known newsreader of the time and certainly for many years after the war, as I can recall him reading the news on the radio, at least up until I was in my early teens. Initially it appears this may have involved a daily ferrying operation from the Capital, but I doubt this would have been the situation for the duration of the hostilities, and logically I would have thought that by 1942 the news operation would have reverted back to London, with the bombing ceasing.

In the January of this year, the government introduced a 100% excess profits tax, effectively cancelling out any sort of racketeering, this of course also had the effect of curtailing traffic deliberately. Having previously mentioned the amount of work that SM covered during these times having a London bias, in this year they were engaged in moving prisoners, not POW's at this stage, from London's prisons to locations elsewhere. Quite what the facts surrounding this type of work were, I have not been able to ascertain, and research I have undertaken appears to imply the prisons remained operating as normal and were not evacuated. However, Beesley's daughter clearly remembers as the 'Blitz' continued South Midland coaches were involved in moving inmates, and on one particular movement this involved many coaches and Holloway prison. William Beesley supervised the task, and she remembers him referring to the 'stench of the female prisoners', so much so that it is believed he had the coaches fumigated on return to the depot at Oxford. In the October the London-Oxford service was reduced to four daily departures in each direction, but Worcester was only served at the weekend.

1942 was a sort of neutral year in many ways, the war continued unabated, though it now looked a possibility, but by no means a certainty, that Great Britain would not necessarily be overrun by the Germans, though the tide had not yet turned in the Country's favour by any means. South Midland were now very much involved in moving military personnel, largely RAF, about the country, and in the immediate area of Oxford alone there were twenty five RAF establishments, nearly all airfields. However, already with a reduction in the number of express journeys allowed, more bad news followed in the June of this year, when the Worcester-London service had to be withdrawn completely, and on the remaining four daily journeys to London the operation of duplicates was banned, leaving effectively only 130 seats now only available daily.

RAF Establishments around Oxford were:- Abingdon, Akeman Street, Barford St John, Brize Norton, Broadwell, Brockton, Chalgrove, Chipping Norton, Culham, Enstone, Finmere, Grove, Haddenham, Harwell, Henley-on-Thames, Kelmscot, Kiddington, Kidlington, Kingston Bagpuize, Milton,

Mount Farm (Dorchester), Pershore, Shellingford, Stanton Harcourt, Upper Heyford, Watchfield and Weston-on-the-Green

Things were happening rapidly now, with an acute shortage of fuel, operators themselves short of vehicles and parts and company staff all over the country overworked. In August the reductions continued with three journeys daily to London, and of course it was only a matter of time, and that came about on the 30th September, when the Oxford-London express service was discontinued. Government orders actually suspended all express services from the 1st October 1942, in the case of South Midland, the RTC insisted the Company's organisation was maintained and suitable work transferred to SM. I suppose this was hardly surprising given South Midland had already been involved with its vehicles on other work than scheduled services, much of it at the instigation of the RTC. Immediately City of Oxford Motor Services local contract work was transferred, and as COMS was suffering acute staff shortages, this ensured essential contract services could be maintained and no doubt the large Ordnance Factory at Didcot was one such contract.

The South Midland coaches worked hard throughout the war years, including the pair of Harrington-bodied Leyland 'Cub' SKPZ2-types.

However, the growing business that would involve SM coaches travelling the length and breadth of the country over the next few years, especially during 1943 and 1944 and accounting for the majority of mileage operated, was that of the movement of Prisoners of War. With a figure that would

89

eventually exceed one thousand POW camps on this island, it was not hard to understand how that part of the business would become so intense.

POW camps in South Midland's operating territory were:- Bicester (5 camps), Bourton-on-the-Hill, Burnham (Slough), Devizes, Didcot, Eastleigh, Evesham, Eynsham, Gloucester, Lambourn, Leckhampton, Malmesbury, Nettlebed, North Hinksey, Pangbourne, Pershore, Purton, Shrivenham, Southampton, Spencers Wood (Reading), Stratford-on-Avon, Swindon, Tewkesbury, Thatcham, Wheatley, Winchcombe, Winchester and Worcester. Possibly included were out of area camps at Aldershot, Bagshot, Bordon, Camberley, Farnham, Norton Fitzwarren (Taunton) and Rugby.

During January 1944 William Beesley and William Taylor, in the light of a probable victory for Great Britain in the long bloody conflict, met at the Hyde Park Hotel, Knightsbridge in London to consider post-war policy. In brief, they considered seriously to sell South Midland, but retain the Gloucester Green café and the High Street office in Oxford. They believed the whole express licensing system would be re-evaluated after the war was over, and the railways would possibly be nationalised. The latter would then contend that in the majority of instances where an express coach service existed, they as an organisation would be able to cope, and the need for such a service would then not exist. They further considered that to ensure this became policy and achieve its aim, this could also include the nationalisation of road transport.

The war years had seen record profits for South Midland and with the perceived 'sword of demacles' hanging over SM's head, and falling vehicle values, informal talks having been ongoing with Red & White periodically over 'forty four and into 'forty five. With Victory in Europe Day on the 8th May 1945 South Midland formally sent an auditors report to Red & White on the 28th May 1945, the decision to sell having finally been taken.

Following the sale of SM William Beesley would involve himself in several ventures thereafter at varying times, all outside of the transport industry, but according to Pat his daughter these at best were only moderately successful. Although William seemed to have lost the Midas touch that he permanently appeared to have throughout the South Midland years, it was much to his credit that he left a well-liked Company with a reputation second to none both locally in Oxfordshire and much further afield, much respected by operators both large and small throughout the land.

Chapter Fourteen   A New Era

On October 8th 1945 Red & White added South Midland to their ever increasing portfolio of Companies, the purchase price paid £46,695.00d, which included sixteen vehicles and both the café and High Street premises. The board of the company was made up of J H Watts (Chairman), Guy Bown (Vice-Chairman), F W Hodgkinson (Managing Director), A J Watts (Technical Engineering Director) and D Lloyd Jones (Director and Secretary), all based at the R & W Head Office at The Bulwark in Chepstow, in those days in the county of Monmouthshire (now Gwent). The last member of the board, but by no means least, was G Nowell who as the Director and General Manager of South Midland was based at Oxford and responsible for the day-to-day operation of the company.

Red & White soon set about repainting and general refurbishment of the war-weary fleet. 'Tiger' TS7 No.35 (BWL 349) is seen amongst the London bomb-sites on a layover in its new red, white and black livery. Note the 'D' suffix after the fleet number to signify it had a diesel engine.

Gerald Nowell had been a RASC lorry driver in World War One, turning to London pirate bus work as The Orange Bus after a short period in the Foreign Office including a spell in Africa. He eventually sold the bus business to London General and commenced another company Great Western Express in October 1928, operating an express coach service between London and Cardiff via Oxford, Cheltenham, Gloucester and Monmouth. Gerald sold out to the Red & White concern in 1932, was retained as a Director and became instrumental in expanding the haulage division of the business. During this period he also started up a taxi operation from December 1937 and a travel agency in London, complete with a Paris agent. His Directorship ceased in 1939 and from October 1940 he served in the RAOC returning to Red & White at the end of the war with responsibility to reorganise R & W's London operations until appointed a Director once again, this time with the newly acquired South Midland.

Gerald Nowell

It was obvious to most individuals involved in passenger transport, that as things began to settle down and military personnel returned home to be demobbed and life returned, albeit very slowly, to some sort of normality, that there would be an ever increasing urge to travel, whether it was to the local cinemas and dance halls or further to perhaps a theatre or the coast. That there was a chronic shortage of vehicles was perhaps very much understating the position. Starved of new vehicles, and in the latter years of the war even the simplest of spare parts, would create serious operational problems for all operators. Gerald Nowell knew the Oxford operation required many additional vehicles, and it was believed that at least fourteen more were needed just to resume a normal express service.

Another recent repaint captured by the camera in the back streets around Victoria Coach Station was the TS4 'Tiger' No.32 (JO 4789), which by then was sporting a longer 'Cov-Rad' replacement radiator.

It appears that four Leylands had been ordered in December of this year, though only one would eventually appear, and that not until over a year later. During the latter part of the year discussions had taken place between R & W and Black & White, I would assume at B & W's instigation, to try and facilitate a share of the profits of the Gloucester Green café. Having regard to the huge potential business B & W could see was about to come South Midland's way, which was quite a cheek actually! The figure that Black & White had suggested was 25%. However this proposed arrangement was never to see the light of day, as further talks on the matter were cancelled in April 1946.

Into 1946 things began to move and with the re-opening of Victoria Coach Station on the 22nd March express coach services recommenced. Authority for a return to full pre-war service having been granted to South Midland, on the 16th April seven journeys Monday to Saturday and five on Sundays commenced to London. The timetable was that introduced in 1932 and without change had carried on until war broke out, again this timetable would see out this decade without alteration. Thirteen AEC 'Regal' 0662 chassis were ordered by R & W for allocation to South Midland, delivery reportedly given as reasonably quick, and this would turn out to be an accurate statement, surprising given that everyone was placing orders for new vehicles, many of them very large from the combines. Perhaps R & W's position as one of the large independents probably also carried weight in the 'pecking' order, whilst Duple received the coach body order.

The possibility of running double-deckers on the London express service was seriously considered at the beginning of this year, a very positive move in respect of 'moving the crowds', but the reason for this not being pursued is not clear. It was most likely to do with the acute delivery delays of new chassis and bodies, and I guess the vehicles would have had coach seats and front entrance. As the seats on the London service were pre-booked, in theory only one man would have been needed, the driver, and this may have been the proposal in the boardroom at Chepstow. However, such a move would have been rejected outright by the Union, now beginning to be a force to be reckoned with, COMS in this year having found out the hard way by a four week strike.

Into the summer of 'forty six saw the re-introduction of the Southsea express route, this now being a seasonal service only operating from Easter to the end of September, departures ex-Oxford 08.30am and 01.30pm (from Worcester at 09.15am) and departures Southsea at 01.30pm (through to Worcester) and 06.00pm to Oxford. In September it was confirmed that one new Leyland would be joining South Midland in the following year, but a second-hand body was to be placed on the chassis as Duple was quoting two-year delivery times. R & W had actually cancelled an order placed by Beesley for a Harrington body, certainly a case of cutting your nose off to spite your face.

The Leyland, of the new 'Tiger' PS1 type, arrived in the October of this year and was dispatched to the R&W-associated bodybuilder Mumford in Lydney, an offshoot of the well known Plymouth based concern. There it received a 1936 body formally fitted to a North Western Bristol JO5G. The thirty five seats of the Eastern Counties Omnibus Company (later Eastern Coach Works) body were of the high backed type, common to that concern, although by now could hardly be described as luxurious, although the body itself retained the sliding roof. The year finished with traffic increasing steadily with the pressure to travel from the public about to erupt.

Shortage of bodybuilder capacity led to the acquisition and refurbishment of a number of older ECOC bodies by R&W. However, the strangest use was for this brand new Leyland 'Tiger' PS1 chassis which became No.38 (LWL 995) in the South Midland fleet in February 1947. Although it was often found on SM's contract operations, it also appeared on the express services as seen above.

Nineteen forty seven commenced, and came in like a lion, the weather was atrocious, to such an extent that many roads became impassable for weeks throughout the country, vehicles of all types having to be abandoned, again in some instances for weeks at a time, this was to be the picture from the January right through to the March. From talking to a couple of South Midland drivers employed at the time, as far as they can recollect, in the main apart from delays varying in length according to the weather of the day, the Oxford-London service was never seriously disrupted, however the Oxford-Worcester service was another matter appearing to be very hit and miss, and certainly on the section of route near Broadway which had a notorious steep hill, often meant that the service made it as far as the hill.

One of the drivers, Arthur Langridge, on several occasions related how often at this point if the hill was not completely blocked by snow, but nonetheless very icy, he would descend it at less than normal walking speed, but had the knack of every few yards nudging the coach into the kerb, this bringing the coach to a halt, without use of the brakes, and slowly but surely he was able by this means to complete the descent without serious problem. Quite what a few of his passengers may have thought one can only guess, but I gather in these immediate post-war years these sort of efforts were greeted with applause, I guess better than spending the night in the wilds at the whims of the weather, especially as another blizzard may have visited during the night. Yes, alternatively, the coach could possibly have made it back to Oxford, but the passengers would wish to get to their destination if possible, and the peoples of this land were now a hardened bunch, prepared to take chances without thinking too long about the consequences as a result of their wartime experiences.

United Counties started to advertise their London express service from Oxford, although only in the month of January, eight departures daily Monday to Saturday in each direction, with six on a Sunday. However, neither SM nor UC would find it necessary to advertise their respective express services to the Capital again during this decade, 1947 –1951 the boom years of express operation. Fares were the same for both companies at 5/6d single, 7/- day return and 10/- period return and fuel rationing would last until during the summer of this year. It was also decided all vehicle overhauls for South Midland would now to be carried out by the very competent employees of the R & W associate company Newbury & District, where new garage and workshops had recently been provided.

United Counties it seemed had only just woken up to the fact in January of this year that Red & White had purchased South Midland. With all the weather problems right at this point I'm a little surprised it even entered the Company's mind, considering in excess of a year had passed since purchase. However from the UC viewpoint R & W had breached the conditions of the Associated Motorways agreement, and of course their own designs on this company. If you reference back several chapters to that agreement, it was in fact true that R & W having purchased SM should then have offered it to the members of Associated Motorways, AM then having the right to buy it from R & W. You can see from where UC was coming, as they had missed out on the deal to merge the two Oxford operations, had this process been followed at the very least UC could have canvassed other AM members, so that AM bought South Midland, it then would have obviously been decided as UC were already in Oxford, that company should operate the Oxford express services to London. Albeit it would probably have meant all the Oxford-London express services under the AM umbrella, but UC could have taken some satisfaction that they were the operating company. One assumes simply R & W told UC where to get off, and UC had difficulty in finding interest amongst other AM members regarding the matter with their pre-occupation with post-war rebuilding.

1ˢᵗ April saw the Worcester arrival / departure point changed from All Hallows to the bus station in Newport Street. Another little gem raises its head concerning the digs used by the South Midland crews in Worcester, the overnight stopping place being Mr and Mrs Wood's house at 11, The Butts, Worcester. The accommodation had a two-fold reputation, that of being a great place for being looked after, the Woods receiving much praise for the food they presented to the drivers and the comfort of the surroundings. The other reputation was a bit more foreboding, in that several drivers, and this included Arthur Langridge, after a couple of what he claimed were frightening experiences during the night, were certain the house was haunted. One assumes however the cuisine and the homely atmosphere more than compensated for the ghost, although Arthur did say a couple of drivers would eat at the house, but after would prefer to bed down in their coach.

The Worcester terminus with AEC 'Regal' No.44 (LJO 761) in company with ancient and modern examples from the Midland Red fleet.

Of great significance was the arrival in May of four of the AEC 'Regal' 0662-type, with 33-seat front entrance coach bodies, magnificent looking machines in my opinion, the Duple body of this time in a class of its own. They were numbered 39-42 (LWL 996-999). During May also South

97

Midland gave an indication of which direction the Company intended to expand the business, namely coach tours of 8-day duration. Advertised as a 'De Luxe Trip to the Royal Forest of Dean centred on Newnham-on-Severn', departure dates of 12th and 19th July and the 23rd and 30th August were given, relatively short notice given of these opportunities, most people probably having already booked holidays, the cost being £12-12s-0d each. However, in July it was announced in the press that due to substantial demand for the previously advertised tours, a departure on the 4th October had been added, disproving my theory of short notice instantly. As this was an autumn date this was reflected in the price of £10-10s-0d.

Representing the initial delivery of AEC 'Regals' was No.41 (LWL 998). It is seen at Windsor Central Station on Ascot Race Week duties in 1954, running with Thames Valley fleetnames, but still in original red, white and black livery and it is in very good order for a 7-year old coach.

Excursions were run from the May to both Epsom and Ascot Races and with a penchant for the arts now, a R & W influence here, South Midland ran an all inclusive excursion to Stratford-upon-Avon in the July for the Shakespeare Festival to see 'Romeo and Juliet'. Henley Regatta, including the firework display, was also visited in July. Contract work was not forgotten, and coaches became employed on moving workers engaged in the building and operation of the Atomic Energy Research Establishment at Harwell. With the threat of nationalisation looming quite large now, various organisations were placing advertisements in the newspapers at this time against the idea, including the giant railway companies GWR, LMS, LNER and SR. With South Midland still desperately short of front line coaches it was offered, by way of Newbury & District (although legally on hire from Red & White), two Albion PW65 chassis fitted with Burlingham utility 34-seat front entrance bus bodies. These duly entered service in June and were used exclusively on contract jobs.

Turning to Paul Lacey's book on Newbury & District, we find more about their history. That Company wishing to replace the last of its petrol engined Leyland's in the fleet, had been sent several of the type of Albion's mentioned, these were also legally on hire from Red & White. The fleet numbers on arrival at Newbury were 233, 243, 244, 249 and 251. Fleet numbers 233 and 251 (EM 2723 and EM 2743) were sent on to SM at Oxford, all the vehicles keeping their original R & W numbers. The chassis had been built in 1932 and were owned at that time by MacShanes of Liverpool, and had Roberts rear entrance 35-seat bus bodies mounted on them. When that Company was absorbed into the R & W empire the vehicles were immediately transferred to South Wales, the Albion engines later replaced by 5-cylinder Gardner units. Owing to body deterioration in 1944 they were re-bodied by Burlingham into the different configuration.

There was no let up in new vehicle deliveries, a single Bedford OB with Duple 29-seat front entrance coach body fleet number 43 (LJO 756) arriving in July, whilst in August further three AEC/Duple coaches arrived to the same specification as those delivered in the May, with fleet numbers 45-47 (LJO 758-760). Fleet number 44 was reserved for a second Bedford OB which would arrive later in the year, but was then stored until the start of the season in 1948. The autumn period saw a commencement of vehicle disposals, and perhaps not surprisingly, the Leyland 'Cub's' and 'Cheetah's' were selected over the older 'Tiger' TS7 chassis in the clear out. Both 'Cub's' and one 'Cheetah', Nos.24/5/7, leaving the fleet in the October, the remaining 'Cheetah', No.26, leaving at the end of the year.

November had seen South Midland make an application for a Worcester-Oxford-Brighton route for 1948, also for RAF camps at Brize Norton, Fairford and Abingdon to London. For whatever reason the Brighton application was withdrawn and that for RAF Abingdon to London refused. However, I think it possible probably on appeal or a later application, Abingdon was granted, as SM drivers remember, certainly in 1948 dropping off personnel at Abingdon, having picked them up at the Victoria

99

The summer sunshine gleams off the stylish lines of Duple-bodied 'Regal' No.46 (LJO 759) at Gloucester Green preparing for the run to London.

Coach Station. 1947 had heralded the start of the boom years in coach travel, which had seen insufficient vehicles available to carry the numbers of passengers wishing to travel, demand exceeding supply. The vehicle shortage would continue until towards the end of 1949, this was indeed the Golden Age when the passengers just kept coming and coming and would do so up until about 1951, an exciting if exhausting era to have been employed in the industry.

South Midland staff of 1947 courtesy of Robert Benstead, many of those listed having served for long periods, some over seventeen years, and of course Ted Surman, in at the beginning of the company (with apologies for any name left out). Ernie Mitchell (Duties Clerk), Jimmy Bessell (Garage Foreman), Betty Langstaff and Josie Allnutt (Café Manageress and Deputy), Fred Pickett (Vehicle Cleaner), Miss Andrews, Joan Brogden and Joyce Langridge (High Street office) and the following drivers, Frank Allnutt, Sidney Axe, Ken Boddington, Reg Brindley, Mr Dutson, Bill Dixon (Shop Steward), Sid Ellerfield, Reg Elliott, Norman Filer, Laurie Gill, Arthur Langridge, Paddy Levy, Tom Lynch, George Nell, Johnny Newport, Harry Ransom, Reg Stayte, Ted Surman, John Wilsden and Robert Benstead. The driving staff in particular had been trained to be the ambassadors of the Company from the outset, the quality of their driving and attention to customer needs being paramount to retaining clients.

1948 was to see a complete transformation of the South Midland vehicle fleet, and this would unusually commence before the traditional season start, no doubt fuelled by pent up demand as production came into full swing, operators not in a position to dictate exact dates of arrival of vehicles. In January six AEC 'Regal'/Duple coaches appeared, still to the specification previously delivered, numerically the first, No.48 (LJO 761), may have been delivered the year previous but stored at the end of 'forty seven, the registration following on from the August batch of vehicles. However as the registrations had probably been blocked booked, it may have not arrived until the January of this year and had arrived as a late delivery, following on came Nos.49-52 (MWL 741-744) and 53 (MJO 278). This enabled the utility-bodied Albion saloons to be returned to Red & White.

The AEC 'Regal'/Duple combination soon became the most numerous in the fleet. No.51 (MWL 743) demonstrates the sliding front door fitted to these bodies, whilst the construction of the cab area is absolutely classic.

With fuel rationing having ceased in the summer of 1947 and with additional vehicles now coming on stream, South Midland was again able to cope with private hire parties. A particular a pastime that was now coming into its own was ballroom dancing, which was becoming a serious business, with local, regional and national competitions. The vast majority

The first of the pair of Bedfords was No.43 (LJO 756), seen later in life in Thames Valley livery. Both had originally been earmarked for delivery to the Newbury & District fleet but sent to Oxford due to necessity. However, it would not be long before they were indeed to become N&D vehicles.

of individuals not possessing a car, rail and coach was the only means to get about, but with transporting costumes and the like many local dance couples and organisations found it preferable to book a coach, an area SM picked up many hires from. Three more coaches arrived in time for the season start and four coaches went into service. Also, as already mentioned, Bedford OB No.44 had been stored after delivery in 1947, and March of this year was chosen as the month to bring it out, dust it off it off and to put it on the road. It was joined by the first of the AEC 'Regal' Mark 3's, again with a Duple front entrance thirty three seat coach body.

The Duple body differed from earlier deliveries on AEC chassis, in that the driver's windscreen area was revised and the coach body had five larger side windows over the previous six of the Mark 1 'Regals', which on a personal note I think detracted slightly from the attraction the earlier coachwork had so defined. Fleet No.54 (MJO 664) was allocated to this coach and was joined a month later by No.55 and 56 (MJO 665 and 667) which set the company up well for the increased tour programme it was to operate in this year. To cope with the numerous enquiries that were now coming South Midland's way from the public, covering about everything they could want to know about travelling by coach, be it express services, private hires, excursions, tours etc., it was decided that the Enquiry Office at 118 High Street, Oxford would now open seven days a week from 08.45am-07.30pm to cope with the demand.

South Midland, through of course R & W's diversification policy, were trying new things, quite successfully, such as different all inclusive types of excursions. In the April of this year for instance for 15/6d adults or 9/- for children, you could have travelled to Chessington Zoo, with Red & White's South Midland this embraced going to the circus at the Zoo plus afternoon tea, bearing in mind though average adult weekly wages of £5-£6.0s.0d at this time, not cheap, but different. Again, in a similar vein, although with a choice of inclusions (and it is obvious to see why), for 14/6d you could enjoy a day visiting London the price including a tour of all the famous place names. However, for an extra 12/6d (27/- in total) you were offered an air flight over the capital. Not sure where, geographically, the aircraft took off and landed though, but again given the average wage mentioned I would be surprised if there were many who included the flight.

The revised style of body for the 'Regal' Mk111 chassis had a much wider offside emergency door in order to fit into the 5-bay construction. No.55 (MJO 665) also clearly shows the semaphore signal arm slot over the front wheel arch, fitted in an attempt to reduce the need for hand signals.

Excursions grew generally, both day and half day, from Easter through to the end of September averaging sixteen per month with the exception of August when the figure leapt to fifty five, which was no mean achievement

103

given the commitment to a very busy express service and tours programme. Indeed, many of the express timings to London in this boom period required five to seven coaches during the week and on a Sunday, according to SM drivers of the time, and common place on a Saturday at the height of the holiday season for ten coaches on some departures. The tours programme consisted of two separate 8-day tours, departures for both now every Saturday from the first Saturday in July until the last Saturday in September. One tour was to The Royal Forest Of Dean and the Wye Valley, centred on the Red & White-associated Unlawater Hotel at Newnham-on-Severn, which included the various day excursions undertaken in the eight day period, finishing on the last night with a buffet dance held in the hotel ballroom, all for the price charged £12-12s-0d. The other tour was to Tintern Abbey and The Wye Valley, centred on another R&W-associated hotel, this time the Beaufort Hotel in Tintern. The majority of the itinery was as per the above tour, but the fully inclusive charge at this location was £13-13s-0d, the hotel offering the additional luxury of central heating!

The N&D fleet was also receiving identical AEC 'Regal' coaches during this period and, as can be seen from the above photo, some later exchanges took place between the fleets. No.70 (ERX 937) was originally N&D's 158.

For those who preferred autumn breaks, this year South Midland again provided 8-day tours departing on the 23rd and 30th October centred this time at the Beaufort Hotel in Tintern, but now reflecting the time of year with a fully inclusive price of £7-7s-0d, quite a reduction over the quoted autumn price of the previous year. Throughout the summer from mid May until the end of September a South Midland Tour of Oxford operated daily, having been started in 1947 and proving an overwhelming success, prices from London were a fully inclusive 14/6d for adults and 7/3d for children, effectively the Oxford tour price of 7/6d and 3/9d added to the journey fare. To ensure the tour connection, which commenced at 02.15pm, passengers from London had the option of departure times of either 09.00am or 10.30am but had to return from Oxford on the 05.00pm departure, no option given, except on a Sunday then 07.00pm with no earlier departure time.

The tour proceeded from Gloucester Green then to the Carfax and into St Aldates, where a visit to Christ Church, one of the most famous Oxford Colleges, was made. From boarding the coach again the following places of interest in Oxford were included, Magdalen College, St. Edmund Hall, New College Chapel, Old Bodleian Library, Brazenose College, Sheldonian Theatre, All Souls College, Wadham College and finally Keble College. From the City the coach then left to visit historic Woodstock and the world famous Blenheim Palace before returning to Oxford.

The year had seen the inaugural service between Worcester and Brighton via Oxford commence, jointly operated with Southdown, running only on Saturdays and Sundays, from the beginning of June through to the second weekend of September, with a departure from Oxford at 07.00am reaching Brighton at 12.30pm. The return from Brighton to Oxford would depart Brighton 08.00am arriving Oxford 01.55pm - yes going by the timetable it took twenty five minutes longer, which must be due to transporting all that seaside rock home. The Worcester to Brighton operation would kick in a month later, although still running until the second weekend of September, this departing Worcester 09.00am reaching Oxford at 11.35am, a break of thirty minutes being taken, before departing Oxford at 12.00noon. Brighton would be reached at 05.30pm, with a departure from Brighton at 12.00noon eventually arriving at Worcester at 08.35pm. Generally speaking Southdown would operate up from the south on a Saturday, returning from Oxford on the Sunday, both departures, South Midland running the reverse situation. A period return from Oxford would set you back 20/3d.

Finally in September the last new vehicle to be delivered in this year emerged as yet another AEC 'Regal' Mark III/Duple, as No.57 (NFC 128). But, with no pressure to place the vehicle into service and the winter about to commence, the vehicle was stored until December and then put into

105

service in time for the additional peak period traffic that was generated. This year had seen the ousting of the three Austin K3 coaches 21-23 which had departed the fleet during May, a much longer life for such a vehicle type than would have been had without the interference of war. With the necessary Act passed by Parliament in 1947 for authority to nationalise many industries, including transport operations, and the sale of the Tilling companies to what was now the British Transport Commission, pressure was mounting on all large passenger transport operators to succumb to the Labour Government's 'wishes' of the day and sell to the BTC.

As 1949 dawned this pressure would intensify, but South Midland as an associate company of the giant Red & White Group would go about its business as usual. An increasing part of its workload was the carrying of RAF personnel when on leave to London and of course from London when returning to camp, inevitably this was to and from Fairford, Brize Norton and Benson but not exclusively. Although many of the personnel were conveyed to London, this was essentially to make connections to all parts of the country, not necessarily by coach, more often than not by train once in the city, onward travel had to be arranged by each individual. The procedure apparently was to transport everyone down on a Friday to Victoria Coach Station, the return would entail coaches employed waiting until midnight at Victoria before departing to the various locations, reaching the destinations in the early hours of Monday morning.

Liberty Motors No.7 (HAX 657) was one of a pair of loaned Bedford OB's.

106

Throughout '49 more new coaches would arrive to modernise the fleet further, being further 'Regal' Mk III/Duple combinations. Nos.58 and 59 (NFC 129-130) arrived in May, 60 –62 (NWL 877-879) in June and finally 63-64 (NJO 217-218) in July. Only the May deliveries had the usual 33-seat configuration, the remainder being only seated for 30-seat passengers, generally for use in connection with 8-day tours now being operated. Even with the additional deliveries, SM found itself very short of vehicles, to the extent that Liberty Motors, another R & W concern, conceded to its masters at Chepstow wishes and loaned two Bedford OB's in the June, these would remain for the rest of the year to help out. These were Liberty Nos.7 and 8 (HAX 657 and 828) and wore a livery of cream and green. Some AEC 'Regals' from that fleet were also proposed for loan, but could not be released before further SM coaches had already been received.

The R & W inspiration for the unusual continued to influence SM in its range of excursions, with a 12-hour cruise off the coast of France, that's right not to France but along the coastline, in early March, one can only hope the weather was good! However, what is clear is that Red & White was not that dissimilar to Beesley's SM, he had always sought to be innovative whenever possible, and had he not sold the business, it is certain similar sorts of experiments with excursions and the like would have been the order of the day. Tours again would make the advertisement headlines, those offered in 1948 repeated this year with the same itinerary and price, but additional departures, commencing every Saturday from the last Saturday in May until the last Saturday in September. However a new 8-day tour was introduced, centred on Porthcawl right on the coast of South Wales. Yet another Group-owned property was used, the Seabank Hotel, but obviously slightly upmarket of the other accommodation owned and used on SM tours, as this vacation would set you back the princely sum of £16-16s-0d.

On the express front, having a desire to forge ties with yet another south eastern operator, along with the continued Worcester-Oxford-Brighton service with Southdown operating again this year, saw also the introduction of the Oxford to Margate service joint with East Kent. This operated in a similar way to the Brighton route, in that again it was confined to Saturday and Sunday operation from June until the beginning of September. One departure daily in each direction, that from Oxford at 07.00am and from Margate at 03.00pm. Of interest is how the coach drivers were rostered on the Worcester-Oxford-London service, which entailed on day one the driver leaving with the 10.15am departure from Oxford to Victoria arriving at 01.03pm. He would then have a break until leaving with the 03.00pm to

Worcester, which would be taken right the way through to arrive at 08.30pm. Day two the coach would leave Worcester at 09.15am arriving in London at 03.18pm, again a break until departing for Oxford at 05.30pm arriving in the city at 08.18pm. Figures available for this year show that express route mileage operated was 256, annual mileage operated 996,442 and passengers carried 339,838 quite remarkable figures for such a small unit of operation. The General Manager, Gerald Nowell, by now was fed up to the back teeth with the threat, as he saw it, of Nationalisation, as he was very anti in his views. It could well be by this time he had an idea of what Red & White intended to do, but in the end he decided to resign from South Midland. He went to Hants & Sussex Motor Services Ltd. towards the close of 1949, but died only a few years later, a bus man if ever there was one. In Nowell's place came L. H. Grimmett, appointed as recently as July 1949 as General Manager of Newbury & District, following the resignation of James Davies as another result of the shadow of Nationalisation. Grimmett had previously served as the R&W Area Manager based at Stroud.

L. H. Grimmett

As the decade drew to a close, yet another era would come to an end also in South Midland's history. Nowell's departure gave credence to the belief that negotiations were taking place between R&W and the BTC towards a sale. What could not be debated was that R&W had never stinted in its responsibility to give SM the best, as the fleet at this time had many coaches of a respectable age and in a good condition, with 24 AEC/Duple coaches alone having been delivered within the space of just 26 months.

Chapter Fifteen   Into the 'Valley

Following the decision of the Directors of Red & White to voluntarily sell their UK bus interests to the nationalised British Transport Commission, the latter organisation found itself with the task of placing those operations within its own structure.

From 1st January 1950 the control of both South Midland and the west Berkshire operator Newbury & District Motor Services Ltd. was placed with the Reading-based Thames Valley Traction Co. Ltd. TV already had its own Dormy Shed in Newbury, but the old N&D and its antecendents had effectively thwarted its plans to expand it that area. TV did, however, share some commonality with South Midland, in that it had two long established express services between Reading and London, as well as Summer express routes to various South Coast towns. The third of the R&W triumvate in the area was Venture of Basingstoke, but it was considered that TV had quite enough on its plate with the other two concerns, so it was assigned to Wilts & Dorset instead.

Typifying the orders for new coaches during the Red & White era was this AEC 'Regal' 111 with Duple 30-seater body received by the new owners in March 1950. The low seating capacity reflects its main role for use on the extended tours programme, and No.65 (OFC 204) is seen at the Beaufort Hotel during a Tintern & Wye Valley tour in red, white and black livery. These coaches represented a considerable investment by the new owners.

These were indeed very significant additions to TV, and contemporary staff recall the substantial additional work involved. In particular, work relating to Road Service Licenses was greatly increased, as all such matters had been dealt with centrally whilst under R&W control. Indeed, Traffic and Engineering Staff were granted a bonus in recognition of the tasks they had faced during the process, whilst an extension to the office accommodation at TV's Head Office at 83 Lower Thorn Street, Reading was put in hand.

A good degree of co-operation between SM and N&D had occurred under R&W, with each fleet often supporting the other in times of need. Under TV the common practice of hiring N&D vehicles to cover peak SM operations continued, whilst the Oxford fleet provided additional coaches for the N&D area when required. N&D's Duple bus-bodied 1947 AEC' Regal' No.136 (DMO 325) is seen leaving Oxford on a London relief duty.

It is not clear how long the BTC had envisaged that the separate identities of these operators might continue, with N&D effectively disappearing after only a couple of years. It soon seems to have become apparent that the good reputation of South Midland as a byword for quality coaching was an asset worthy of retention. On 10th February 1950 a meeting was held at Crewe House, Curzon Street, London W1, when TV appointed new Directors for SM from within its ranks, with the Registered Office being transferred to the Reading address with effect from the following day.

During February the TV Engineer Basil Sutton visited the Oxford garage in Iffley Road and both the Newbury premises in Mill Lane to address future strategy for maintaining the acquired fleets. The Reading Works was very busy coping with keeping TV's own war weary fleet roadworthy, so it was decided that major dockings for both N&D and SM would be dealt with at the Newbury garage which had received considerable investment under R&W. The old TV shed, just some 50 yards away, would be utilised as a paint and body shop for both fleets. As the shed was larger than required for that role, it also became a regular winter store for de-licensed coaches, though TV's large shed at Stokenchurch was also used. Mr. Bessell, who had for some years looked after maintenance at Oxford, was put in charge of day-to-day engineering requirements at Iffley Road, whilst Sid Taylor was Engineer at Newbury, aided by his righthand man Reg Hibbert.

Sutton also made a number of transfers between the two fleets in the interest of standardisation during January 1950. The pair of 1947/8 Bedford OB's 43/4 (LJO 756/7) were sent to Newbury, where their small size made them particularly suitable for the weight-restricted Haying Island excursions and small-capacity private hires. The remaining Leylands active at Oxford, including the rather hybrid 1947 example with a 1936 bus body, were transferred to N&D. The Bedfords became N&D Nos.164/5, whilst former SM Leyland 'Tiger' TS7's 35/6/7 (BWL 349, CWL 951/3) and PS1-type 38 (LWL 995) became N&D 167, 168, 166 and 169 respectively.

The 1947 Leyland 'Tiger' PS1 with its 1936 ECOC body had come about through the difficulties of obtaining new bodies due to post-war shortages.

Also seen after transfer, but back on hire on its old ground at Gloucester Green, is former SM Bedford No.43 (LJO 756) in the guise of N&D No.164. The R&W-style livery particularly suited the Duple coachwork.

In exchange for the Bedfords and the post-war 'Tiger', a trio of N&D AEC 'Regal' coaches new in 1948/9 were transferred to the South Midland fleet. N&D's 149/50 (EJB 649/50) and 158 (ERX 937) all carried the familiar Duple bodywork and became SM Nos.68-70. The Red & White livery was not too different to TV's own scheme, and the vehicle types were familiar.

Transferred from N&D was 'Regal' No.68 (EJB 649) seen at Maidenhead.

After the transfer had taken place the South Midland fleet consisted of 30 Duple-bodied AEC 'Regals' delivered between 1947 and 1950. In addition Leyland Tiger TS7 No.34 (BFC 675) was de-licensed and soon joined other laid-up vehicles at Newbury awaiting disposal or cannibalisation.

SOUTH MIDLAND
MOTOR SERVICES LTD.

118 HIGH STREET & GLOUCESTER GREEN OXFORD
Tel. 4138/9

TRAVEL BUREAU and INFORMATION OFFICE
open 8.45 a.m. to 7.30 p.m. daily (including Sundays)

FOR REGULAR COACH SERVICES TO

LONDON — OXFORD — WORCESTER
MARGATE — BRIGHTON — SOUTHSEA

Eight-day Motor Coach Tours	Day and Half-day Tours	Sightseeing Tours of Oxford

BOOKINGS BY COACH TO ALL PARTS OF BRITAIN

Advert block for South Midland from a local Oxford guidebook of 1950.

As already noted, the future use of the 1947 Leyland 'Tiger' PS1 received consideration, resulting in the decision to have it re-bodied as a coach. New vehicles were hard to obtain, so the potential of this vehicle was not to be missed. As the regulations on PSV's had changed since it was constructed to a maximum width of 8ft and length of 30ft, it was also decided to look at extending the chassis dimensions as well.

At the time Thames Valley was also planning delivery of a batch of coaches with fully-fronted bodies by Eastern Coach Works on Bristol LWL6B chassis. During June 1950 the Engineer visited the Leyland works at Kingston to see a PS2-type 'Tiger' chassis that had been converted from the old 17ft 6ins wheelbase to the new 18ft 9ins. As a result of this visit, it was decided to rebuild 169's chassis to take a 30ft x 8ft body. The chassis width of 7ft 6ins would be retained in common with other new examples in the interim period of the change in regulations, together with many of those vehicles being re-bodied during that time. It was seen as particularly desirable to have a 'new' coach for the anticipated extra excursions that the forthcoming Festival of Britain would generate during 1951. The old ECOC body was sold for £10 to Mr. Shirley of Darby Green, Blackwater, Surrey, being dropped from the chassis at that location on 5th November 1950. The chassis then proceeded to Reading Works for conversion to the longer wheelbase using the kit obtained from Leyland Motors. TV was of the opinion that the resulting coach would warrant registration as a new vehicle, but Berkshire CC rejected that idea. Indeed, Leyland even confirmed that replacement chassis plates could be supplied if required!

The general difficulty in obtaining new coaches resulted in SM's old TS7 'Tigers' staying with N&D than originally intended. In this view N&D 168 has returned to familiar territory at Gloucester Green, albeit on a relief duty for Associated Motorways – a common aspect of South Midland work. Selected drivers at N&D and SM were also ready with an overnight case packed, ready for a day's driving to any point on the vast network.

Arrangements were made with Eastern Coach Works for a new body to be built on the chassis, the design being adapted from the fully-fronted style then being fitted to Bristol LL/LWL types, some of which retained exposed radiators. However, due to delays at the Lowestoft works, the chassis could not be accepted until early the following year. Also in store that winter was an underfloor-engined AEC 'Regal' IV chassis, an outstanding legacy from R&W orders for the SM fleet, again without any immediate prospect of any

In addition to receiving old 'Tigers' back on a regular basis, similar TS7's were also loaned from Thames Valley, including this 1935 example with Duple 'camel-back' body. Seen in London complete with painted 'on hire' board is TV No.264 (JB 5843), fully refurbished after military service.

Body being built. Finally there was also a quartet of underfloor-engined Guy 'Arab' UF chassis on order for bodies by the R&W-associated Lydney Coachworks in the Forest of Dean. A pair each had been intended for N&D and SM, though TV earmarked all 4 for the Oxford fleet. It should be noted that most coachbuilders of the time had full order books for several years!

TV took on the wider advertising of the SM extended tours, as well as the coastal express facilities. The fleet had generally been quite hard worked, though vehicle requirements were slashed during the winter months, so most major dockings and all scheduled repaints were programmed to suit. The Oxford – Henley – Maidenhead – London route had a mileage of just under 60, whilst the full run from Worcester was almost as far again at 116 miles, and the Summer-only Worcester – Oxford – Newbury – Southsea route was 137 miles. N&D had been the local booking agent for SM since 1932, which had greatly assisted loadings on the Southsea route, including pickup points between Newbury Winchester. Apart from the fleet based at Iffley Road, Oxford, up to 3 coaches were kept at Worcester and 3 more overnight in London for early morning runs.

The new regime for maintenance settled down well, though it did not suit everyone. Sid Taylor, together with fellow old N&D garage hand Edwin Whitington, decided to set up on their own on contract work as Enterprise Coaches. Sid resigned on 9th September, though the new project had been operated 'on the side' for a while before then, purchasing the withdrawn SM Leyland 'Tiger' TS7 No.34 (BFC 675) as part of his new venture.

Reg Hibbert took Taylor's place as Engineer, and the fine condition of both the Newbury and Oxford fleets throughout the 1950's and 1960's was a testament to his high standards. One practice instigated by Reg at both depots was that a bucket of black paint was always on hand for night staff to touch up any damage to mudguards before return to service the next day!

During mid-September a meeting took place between TV and Maidenhead Corporation regarding the provision of land for an off-road coach station in the town. There was no doubt that such a facility was needed, as the TV bus station in Bridge Avenue could not handle the numerous relief coaches then commonplace at peak times, many of them on the South Midland Oxford – London service. A large vacant plot of land at nearby York Avenue was made available for the purpose and the sale was duly arranged. In response to this, TV also agreed to build a new Enquiry Office and extend the café.

The Gloucester Green, Oxford enquiry office with its extensive displays for the extended tours, local tours and nationwide coach rxpress bookings.

Chapter Sixteen   Festival Days

Post-war Britain had still yet to shake off the austerity it had suffered for over a decade, so for the Summer of 1951 the Government planned a large exhibition and celebrations to herald the dawn of a new era of prosperity. The year was also of course the centenary of the Great Exhibition of 1851, when the products and cultures of the British Empire were on show.

For SM this would inevitable result in a large increase in traffic on the London routes, together with regular excursions, a return to the busy days of the 1924 Wembley exhibition. However, delivery of new coaches was still proving difficult. The continuing saga of the AEC 'Regal' IV coach, which should have gone to Duple, is typical of the frustrations of that time.

Duple-bodied 1948 AEC 'Regal' No.56 (MJO 667) is seen entering the Gloucester Green terminus to take to duties on the London express route.

Discussions took place with Duple Motor Bodies of Hendon on 13th November 1950, during which it was agreed that this coach would receive an 'Ambassador' type body as soon as the programme allowed. This type featured a centre sliding entrance and deep front windows. On 19th February 1951 the chassis was taken to Duple. However, no work got underway and the situation remained the same through to mid-May, with Duple accepting cancellation of the order on the 16th of that month. The chassis was collected on 21st May and then taken to ECW at Lowestoft on 23rd May. However, Eastern Coach Works were very busy and also short of materials. A new programme of delivery for March 1952 was agreed when the order was confirmed with them in September 1951, the style of body to match the batch of Bristol LS coaches also programmed for the SM fleet.

Despite these difficulties a full programme of excursions and extended tours, together with the customary Summer express services were on offer:-

Express Services

Oxford – Henley – Maidenhead – London   Daily
Worcester – Oxford – Henley – Maidenhead – London   Daily
Worcester – Oxford – Newbury – Winchester – Southsea Daily 1/6 to 30/9
Oxford – Newbury – Winchester – Southsea   Daily 1/6 to 30/9
Oxford – London – Margate (joint with East Kent)   Sats. only 21/7 to 25/8
Worcester – London – Brighton (joint with Southdown) Summer Sats/Suns.
Oxford – London – Brighton (joint with Southdown)   Summer up to Daily
Brighton services could be booked for onward travel by Southdown routes to Hove, Worthing, Lewes, Rottingdean, Seaford etc. with through tickets.

8-day Extended Tours

No.1 Tintern & Wye Valley, centred at the Beaufort Hotel, Tintern
No.2 Symonds Yat & Wye Valley, centred at Wye Rapids, Symonds Yat
No.3 Royal Forest of Dean & Wye Valley centred at the Unlawater Hotel, Newnham-on-Severn

Prices for the above tours, departing	*London*	*M'h/Henley*	*Oxford*
Saturday departures 6/6 to 25/8	*£13.2.9*	*£12.18.3*	*£12.12.0*
Saturday departures 1/9 to 27/10	*£9.19.9*	*£9.15.3*	*£9.9.0*

No.4 Welsh Coast centred at the Seabank Hotel, Porthcawl
Departs Sats. June to Sept. £16.16.0 from London, M'h/Henley or Oxford
No.5 North Devon centred at Collingwood Hotel, Ilfracombe
Departs Thurs. June to Sept. £17.17.0 from London, M'h/Hen. or Oxford

All tours are fully inclusive, covering full hotel accommodation, gratutities, motor coach tours to beauty spots, teas on route – there are no extras.

Sight-seeing Tour of Oxford

Summer daily until end of September at 15 shillings for adults, half fare for children, inclusive of travel from London. Connecting coaches leave at 9am and 10.30am from London (Victoria Coach Station), returning from Oxford at 5pm and 7pm.

AEC 'Regal' No.60 (NWL 877) of 1949 is seen at the coach park near the Southsea funfair and pier on the very popular Summertime express route.

As noted in the previous chapter, the N&D Leyland 'Tiger' PS1 chassis was ready for re-bodying, and it finally departed for Lowestoft on 27th February 1951, with fingers crossed that it would return without delay!

However, it was still without the return of this vehicle that opening of the Festival of Britain by King George VI took place on 3rd May 1951. The main arena for the festival was the complex of buildings constructed in 'futuristic' style on London's bomb-damaged South Bank, though there were also a number of regional events and travelling exhibitions by both road and boat. The trade generated from this event was enormous for SM, leading to the extensive use of hired vehicles from the TV and N&D fleets.

A change in BTC policy on coach livery from 1951 dictated that they should be all-over light cream, relieved only by mudguards painted in the appropriate fleet colour, which would also be applied to future re-paints. So when the Leyland PS1 finally returned on 6th June 1951, it carried the new scheme. However, the vehicle remained a member of the N&D fleet, though it was often to be seen in Oxford on hire to SM, even re-entering that fleet, as we shall see in due course!

Another facet of operation under the BTC was co-operation with railways on road/rail excursions, which had already been a regular feature for the railway-associated Thames Valley in the pre-war era. SM's first venture of this kind occurred on Sunday 2nd September 1951, when 62 passengers were met from a train at Oxford and taken on a tour to Bourton-on-the-Water. The tour was a success and more would be included from 1952.

From 22nd February 1952 a new Management Agreement between TV/N&D/SM introduced common controls to ease the accounting processes etc. However, the more pressing issue was still the continued delays for delivery to new coaches. The completion of the 4 Guys was still uncertain due to problems with the Lydney bodies. An inspector from ECW, working on behalf of the BTC, was not satisfied with the standard of work. In due course the part-completed vehicles were driven over to the BTC-associated Brisington Body Works in Bristol for completion.

Equally exasperating was the wait for the 6 Bristol LS6G's and the AEC 'Regal' IV being bodied at ECW. Every month Engineer Sutton received a note with revised delivery dates, and a read through the correspondence of the period shows just how frustrating it was for all parties! In order to partly overcome this situation, arrangements were made to loan a pair of 1-month old Leyland 'Royal Tiger' coaches with Lydney 41-seater bodies from Red & White, so their Nos.UC951 and UC2051 (JWO 213 and JWO 546) were operated from May to November 1952.

Red & White No.UC2051 is seen on loan working on the London express.

Despite this background, SM actually made a significant acquisition from 1st May 1952, with the BTC having decided to transfer the United Counties Oxford – High Wycombe – London route to it. This service had originated with Varsity Express in October 1929, which at the time had been a thorn in the side of SM due to the inevitable fares-war.

With this route came 8 Bristol L-series vehicles fitted with ECW bodies, which was indeed fortunate. These were quite a varied collection, having been built between 1948 and 1951, becoming SM Nos.71/2 (EBD 234/5), both L6B's with DP31R bodies, Nos.73/4 (EBD 236/7), both L6B's with fully-fronted (but with exposed radiator) FC31F bodies, together with Nos.75-8 (FRP 832/3/4/6) with LL6B chassis and 8ft wide FC37F bodies.

No.71 (EBD 234) is seen in service still in UCOC green and cream 'express' livery. The pair of these dual-purpose vehicles was sold to TV in February 1953, once deliveries of new coaches permitted their release.

Also as part of the UCOC deal was its garage in Botley Road, Oxford, and that site would duly be expanded, as it was preferable to the SM garage in Iffley Road. The former UCOC coaches had their green mudguards repainted red in due course, though the dual-purpose L6B's remained green and cream until transferred to TV. In due course UCOC also decided to end its programme of extended tours, and enquirers were directed to those of South Midland, which could be accessed at Oxford, London and Wycombe.

The other L6B's from UCOC carried this 'interim' style of full-fronted body, and No.74 (EBD 237) is seen on the Oxford sightseeing tour not long after acquisition. Note the split style of South Midland fleetname then used.

The first of the underfloor-engined Bristol LS6G coaches arrived in June 1952 as Nos.79-81 (SFC 565-7), SM still retaining its own fleet number series and its vehicles being registered in Oxford. These were followed by the AEC 'Regal' IV No.85 (SFC 571) in July, the body of which had only a few minor differences to the LS's in order to accommodate filler caps etc.

Bristol LS No.80 (SFC 566) posed outside the Blue Coat School, Sonning.

Although the underfloor-engined 'Regal' carried the ECW 'wings' on the front panel, the opportunity was not taken to place an AEC triangular badge there. Reports from contemporary drivers concerning this vehicle rate its performance on a par to the LS's, but somewhat lighter to handle, and as such the vehicle was destined to put in a full-length career at Oxford. The AEC and the batch of Bristols were fitted with driver's public address, whilst it is worth noting that the latter were originally allocated Nos.71-6.

The remaining LS's did not arrive until October, as Nos.82-4 (SFC 568-70), and their delay caused TV to transfer 6 chassis from its 1953 allocation for bodying as coaches for SM to ensure more vehicles would be available.

Only very minor details made the body on the AEC 'Regal' IV different from those fitted to the Bristols, with the split windscreen being the only means of distinguishing this particular coach from a distance. In this view the original trafficator arms have been replaced by flashers, but see the photo of Bristol LS on page 122 for their original position.

The long-awaited Guys started to arrive in March with No.88 (SFC 503), followed by Nos.86/9 (SFC 501/4) in April, then finally No.87 (SFC 502) in May. Note that their registrations were actually earlier than the LS's and AEC that preceded them, another sign of false optimism of their delivery! These were particular heavyweight vehicles, partly because of having a full chassis as opposed to the semi-chassisless Bristol, but all the same they did

Guy No.88 (SFC 503) seen in original condition at the newly-opened coach station in Maidenhead. The Leyland 'Royal Tiger' inspiration for the body style is very evident. Note the Guy badge on the front panel.

weigh in at 8tons 5cwt 3qtr compared with the LS at 7tons, and even a Bristol KSW double-decker at 7tons 17cwt! The consequent higher running costs must have counted towards their relatively short career with SM.

A pair of hired coaches in Summer 1952 at Gloucester Green, with TV No.388 (BMO 987), a 1939 Harrington-bodied Leyland 'Tiger' TS8 in green livery, with Red & White 'Royal Tiger' No.UC2051 (JWO 546).

On 18th March the Board approved plans to extend the ex-UCOC Botley Road garage to make fuller use of the site. Bringing the capacity up to 41 under cover and 7 outside, though the Iffley Road premises were retained.

The delivery situation showed some improvement, with the Bristol LS6B's appearing from June 1953 as Nos.90-2 (TWL 55-7), followed in July by 93 (TWL 58) and 94/5 (TWL 59/60) in August and October respectively.

Botley Road garage seen after the extensive additions of 1953/4.

On the services front, the Summer of 1952 had seen the addition of a through express from Oxford to Eastbourne, operated jointly with Southdown Motor Services on Saturdays between June and September. Two more tours were added for 1952, these being South Devon, based at the Haldon Manor Hotel, which departed on Wednesdays for 8 days, and a Heart of England tour actually based at the Melville Hotel, Oxford, running on Sundays at 7 days duration. As a result of the acquisition of the UCOC London route, all tours were now advertised with connections from High Wycombe, where of course TV had 2 large garages and numerous services. For 1953 an 8-day Cornwall tour was added, based at the Fistral Bay Hotel, Newquay, whilst on the express front a Saturdays-only June to September route to Hastings and Bexhill, joint with Maidstone & District was started.

125

The Company also operated an extensive programme of excursions, and the leaflet for June 1952 shows a good selection of both local and more distant destinations and events, with the following being covered:-

Ascot Races	*Banbury*	*Boulters Lock*
Bournemouth	*Bourton-on-the-Water*	*Brighton*
Buckingham	*California-in-England*	*Clevedon*
Compton Wynyates	*Golden Valley*	*Lechlade*
Malvern Hills	*Marlow*	*Newbury Races*
Pangbourne	*Savernake*	*Shakespeare tour*
Southend	*Weston-super-Mare*	*Whipsnade Zoo*
Wye Valley	Fares varied from 5shillings to 12s 6d	

However, the major event of 1953 was the Coronation of Queen Elizabeth II on 2nd June at Westminster Cathedral. The event drew huge crowds, with the inevitable increase in the use of the express services and private hires. In order to cope with the demand for those wishing to get into position along the coronation route, and also those wanting to stay on to enjoy the celebrations afterwards, extra journeys were added on both services between Oxford and London. Extra capacity was also available between London and Maidenhead on the Thames Valley Route B if required.

The 1953 deliveries of Bristol LS coaches varied in detail from the previous examples, having no roof quarter-lights, two-piece front windscreens, and by having the fuel and water filler caps on their nearside instead.

Chapter Seventeen   And The Winner Is...

TV No.389 (BMO 988), a 1939 Harrington-bodied 'Tiger' TS8 in its final livery of red and cream, is seen at Newbury Wharf acting as relief on the South Midland express service to Southsea. Many of this batch of 10 coaches were extensively used on SM duties throughout the early 1950's until withdrawn in October 1954, being sold for export to Yugoslavia!

By 1954 operations were on a very settled pattern, which reflected the general situation in the industry. Indeed, it was a very busy but profitable era for bus and coach operators. Inevitably, though, there would be trials and tribulations yet to come, and the mid-1950's was to see a foretaste of things to come.

However, in the meantime, the business of meeting demand saw a number of TV coaches on hire extensively throughout the year, there being no more new additions to the SM fleet during 1954-7. With the transfer of the SM Road Service Licenses to TV during 1954, it must have made some think that the days of the separate identity might soon disappear? For the 1954 touring season the only change was the deletion of the Forest of Dean & Wye Valley tour, which had operated during Spring and Autumn only.

By September 1954 some of the earlier AEC 'Regals' were in need of some refurbishment internally, so it was decided that 12 would be selected for a thorough overhaul at ECW. No.41 (LWL 998) left for the trip to Lowestoft

The AEC's were also re-painted into the cream and red livery, which made them looked quite different, the old livery having been in harmony with the lines of the Duple coachwork. No.46 (LJO 759) is seen at Victoria.

in October, followed by Nos.40, 47 and 51 (LWL 997, LJO 760 and MWL 743) in November, then 42 (LWL 999) in January 1955, 45/6 (LJO 758/9) in February, 48-50/2/3 (LJO 761, MWL 741/2/4 and MJO 278) in March, April, May, June and July respectively. Each was away for between 2 and 4 months, during which time they were also re-seated to take 35 passengers.

Thames Valley got a new General Manager from 1st January 1955, when Tom Pruett was appointed. He had previously served with Brighton, Hove & District Omnibus Co. Ltd., which was notable for not having operated coaches. This fact was to have a bearing on the SM story, as Mr. Pruett let the TV coach fleet decline over the years, though he left SM intact. In fact he was of the opinion that TV should concentrate its resources on the bus operations, particularly as the industry entered a difficult phase of increased costs and industrial unrest. He also believed that excursions from TV's area should be left to the independents – indeed, it was rumoured that he even bought shares in Smith's Luxury Coaches of Reading in due course!

As already noted, TV coaches were frequently on loan to Oxford, but from 1955 a steady flow of vehicles from the parent fleet were transferred to SM.

The first of these were two 1950 Windover-bodied Bristol L6B's, 548 (FMO 23) and 553 (FMO 935), both of which were transferred in January. Although the SM coaches were being repainted into the cream livery, none of this Windover-bodied Bristols wore that phase of SM livery, retaining their original red and cream instead.

For the Summer of 1955 yet another South Coast through destination was provided with a Saturday-only connection, this time Worthing, which was worked jointly with Southdown MS. On the tours front, a new Central Wales tour was added, centred at the Glen Usk Hotel in Llandrindod Wells.

Windover-bodied Bristol 553 (FMO 935) after transfer to South Midland. It is seen at Gloucester Green in company with Beadle-bodied Royal Blue Bristol coach 1231 (HOD 33) bound for Portsmouth via Reading.

No significant changes were made to any of the seasonal coastal expresses for 1956, but a number of amendments were made to the extended tours, with changes of hotel for Cornwall (now the Bay Hotel, Newquay) and South Devon (now the Warberry Hotel, Torquay). The Heart of England tour based at Oxford had not been well supported and was dropped, there being a new English Lakes tour, based at the Grand Hotel, Grange-over-Sands added instead.

However, the company duly found itself having to restrict mileage on its London express reliefs and excursions programme, following the Suez Crises from July to November 1956, when Egypt seized the Suez Canal and disrupted oil supplies.

One of the effects emanating from Tom Pruett's reign at TV had been the introduction of an open-top double-deck 'riverside' service between Reading and Maidenhead (later also Windsor). This had started in April 1956, but the success was only limited, partly due to the poor weather that Summer. As a result, it was decided that for 1957 the route would start later in the Summer, leading to one of the quartet of ex-BH&D Bristol K5G's being surplus to requirements, which in turn gave an opportunity to try something at Oxford instead. It was decided to license the Oxford Colleges tour to include nearby Blenheim Palace and to use the open-topper on it from August!

1940 Bristol K5G No.770 (CAP 206) carried an ECW body that had been heavily rebuilt in BH&D's workshops. It is seen at Gloucester Green on the Colleges and Blenheim Palace tour, fortunately on one of the drier days!

Although the addition of this vehicle, SM's first double-decker, was a good move, the Summer was unfortunately a rather wet one, resulting in the cessation of use of all the open-toppers on 31st August. From that date the SM example was placed in store at Oxford, the duty being covered by a coach for the remainder of the season.

Just a little earlier, the Company had suffered the first of a number of strikes by its crews that were to mark this unsettled period for the industry, with a strike call for 20th-27th July 1957. It was agreed that any extended tours in operation would be completed, but contingency plans were put into

Bristol L6B No.74 (EBD 237) is seen at Tintern on the Wye Valley tour, a duty that increasingly fell to this type as the other 7ft. 6ins vehicles were sold off.

place to have any other tours and excursions covered by vehicles and drivers hired from other operators.

Rationalisation of contract workings led to the transfer to SM from 1st October 1957 of 3 routes to RAF Milton, a couple of miles west of Didcot, from various points north of Newbury. This provided some economies in not having to outstation contract vehicles, but just the following year two of those routes were lost to Reliance Motor Services after the RAF re-tendered them. To make matters worse, the same operator also gained its first license for extended tours from the Newbury area in 1958!

There were no changes to the tours programme during 1957, though initial discussions took place during November for a tour of Southern Ireland for the following season.

At the close of the season it was possible to dispose of some of the AEC 'Regal' coaches, and during October Nos.45, 48, 52 and 62 (LJO 758/61, MWL 744 and MWL 879) were all sold. Wintertime always saw a number of coaches de-licensed, and 16 coaches were put aside that year.

The other subject under consideration at this time was a change of livery, as most acknowledged that the cream scheme did not wear well. It was also recognised that SM was in many ways a distinctive operator, the possibility of absorbtion in TV having apparently been discounted. As it was felt that attractiveness to women might be a key factor, especially for tours bookings, Tom Pruett consulted his wife. She suggested a pink scheme that was not, fortunately, taken up – the vision of a pink MW springs to mind! However, SM did get its very own livery, the choice being maroon and cream, the application of which owed more than a little to the style used by Royal Blue, even down to the beaded fleetname panels.

Although a number of 'Regals' were disposed off from 1957, others were repainted in the new maroon livery, including No.56 (MJO 667).

During early January 1958 a representative of the Republic of Ireland Tourist Board visited the TV offices to meet with TV/SM officials over the planning of the first Eire tour. On 17th of that month an application was made for the license, which included a pick-up point at Cheltenham, in the hope of tapping into the potential connections with Associated Motorways. Although British Railways (Western Region) had agreed not to object to the proposal, pressure from other non-BTC users of Cheltenham ensured that the point was deleted. However, the tour was approved on 5th February, leading to a reciprocal visit to Eire by the Traffic Manager and Traffic

Superintendent (Oxford). Also, on 20th March officials attended a conference at London Coastal Coaches on the future of coach-air touring. Long-serving Mr. Bessell left the post of Depot Foreman, and his place was taken over by Mr. D. Munday from 24th February.

New coaches for 1958 arrived during March and April as Nos.800-3 (ORX 631-4), thereby ending the practice of using a separate series of fleet numbers for SM and registration in Oxford. The first 3 were standard ECW 34-seaters on Bristol MW6G chassis for tours work, whilst the 4th had received extra-special treatment at ECW in preparation for its initial role. Extra features included the chroming of the ECW 'wings', plus a pair of continental-style air-horns on the front dome, whilst the seating was for just 32. All 4 had the front fleetname panel built in with a reduced sized grille.

Coach 803 had been entered for the British Coach Rally at Brighton on 20th April, where it won the *Concours d'Elegance*, much to the delight of all the staff back at Oxford! Driver Langridge also completed the driving course of the judging in immaculate form, much to his credit.

The triumphant coach on its return to Botley Road from the Brighton event. Arthur Langridge proudly holds the cup. The award was quite an achievement for a heavyweight like the MW, but the presentation of the vehicle, the skills of the driver, and perhaps the new livery all helped.

Above - The interior of MW coach No.803 (ORX 634). Note the high level of glazing and the 'SM' monograms on the headrest covers. Below - Coach 803 stands on the right at Harrogate, with the winning cup in front. It shares the display with other new deliveries of Bristol MW and 'Lodekka' variants, plus an older Bedford OB converted by Lincolnshire RCC to a new role for the Skegness seafront operation.

The winning coach was sent to West Yorkshire's Harrogate depot for display in connection with the conference of Tilling Group & Scottish Omnibuses companies held there on 25th April. Following its return home, it went on display, complete with tours placards and brochures, going to Maidenhead on 30th April, followed by Newbury on 1st May and Reading on 2nd May. As a final curtain call before taking up its touring duties, it was presented to BTC Chairman Sir Brian Rolerston on 8th May.

With such a buzz at Oxford, the next arrival must have been quite a surprise! As the negotiations over the Eire tour took shape, it was decided to ask the Republic's state-owned Coras Iompair Eireann to take care of the coach during its season over-the-water. CIE already had a large fleet of Leyland types, but none of the Bristols making up the SM touring fleet. So, after an absence of 8 years, the 1947 'Tiger' PS1 found its way back to the SM fleet!

Leyland 'Tiger' PS1 No.169 (LWL 995) returned to SM in June 1958 in the new maroon livery. This coach had been new to SM in 1947 (with a 1936 body), transferred to N&D 1950, re-bodied as shown above in 1951, re-lettered as TV around 1952, being finally returned to Oxford once again!

The first Eire tour commenced on 18th June, with the coach leaving Oxford for Fishguard for the overnight sailing to Rosslare. On 19th the party went on to Tramore, on the 20th to Glengarriff, with all day of the following day there. The fifth and sixth days were spent on day tours of the Ring of Kerry and Killarney, returning each night to Glengarriff. On 23rd Cobh was reached, then the following day Cork and Blarney Castle were visited en route to Rosslare for the overnight ferry back to Fishguard, onward travel to Oxford being completed on the 25th. The tour was covered by Driver Langridge and proved very successful.

No further new coaches came to SM in 1958, but a quartet of 1953/4 Bristol LS6B coaches were drafted in from the Thames Valley fleet. These were Nos.689/90/2/3 (HMO 835/6/8/9), transferred for express and general duties, their move signalling the start of a reduction in the TV coach fleet under Tom Pruett. The four carried C39F bodies and were transferred to SM during June. 692, it should be said, was not continuously at Oxford, though it retained SM fleetnames, as it spent sometime away at Reading during its 6 years in that fleet.

Bristol LS6B No.689 (HMO 835) after re-painting into the new SM livery. It should be noted that the TV coaches were also given the same scheme in due course, prompting speculation that all coaches would run as SM!

The receipt of more LS's permitted the disposal of further AEC 'Regals' in July, with the departure of Nos.39, 40 and 42 (LWL 996/7/9), followed by ex-N&D No.69 (EJB 650) during August.

During October 1958 Bristol MW6G No.803 (ORX 634) was re-seated to the standard touring pattern of 34, its 'showtime' now being over, though the roof-mounted air horns were retained.

The Summer express services to Hastings and Bexhill had not reached a level to make them worthwhile retaining, so they were discontinued after the 1958 season. On the tour front, a new 10-day Scottish tour was introduced, based at the Atholl Palace Hotel in Pitlochry.

Further AEC 'Regals' were ousted in October, with the departure of Nos.41 (LWL 998), 46/7 (LJO 759/60) and 49/50 (MWL 741/2), which were followed in December by Nos.53-5 (MJO 278 and MJO 664/5) and 60 (NWL 877), whilst the open-top K5G was placed in store for the Winter.

A very bad accident befell Guy coach No.87 (SFC 502) when it was being driven down to Newbury empty at 9.45pm on 26th June 1958 to cover a 41-seater private hire. Driver Ray Bailey saw a man on an unlit cycle come into his headlights and swerved to avoid him. The resulting skid on a very wet surface led to the coach continuing across the road, where it struck a building with such a force that it collapsed, trapping the cyclist under the front wheels. The scene that greeted a cursing Reg Hibbert, called from his home to the recovery, was one of a coach halfway up the ground floor wall, with bricks strewn all around, heavy lifting tackle having to be brought in!

How No.87 looked in the clear light of the following day! Fortunately for the driver, the heavy chassis had given him enough protection from serious injury, though it had done as good a job as the demolition man's ball on the hapless building! The body was rebuilt to the original style at Newbury.

Above - Former N&D AEC 'Regal' No.147 (EJB 147) duly gained Thames Valley fleetnames, but in this view it is seen at Gloucester Green on hire to SM. Several of SM's 'Regals' also spent a period around 1954 running at Newbury and Reading with TV fleetnames. Below – As the various batches of coaches got the new livery, it had the effect of altering their 'character', as shown by Bristol LL6B No.75 (FRP 832), when the darker sides emphasised the sweep of the beading. Other features to note on this ex-United Counties example are the side windows and the overhang caused by the combination of a 7ft 6ins chassis and the 8ft wide ECW body.

Chapter Eighteen   Fifties into Sixties

January 1959 saw the acquisition of further coaches from United Counties, all being Bristol LL6B's. These became Nos.821-7 (FRP 835/7-42), all being from the same batch already represented by the take-over of 1952. In their case the 1951 chassis had subsequently been fitted with 8ft.-wide axles to match the fully-fronted 37-seater ECW bodies of that width. Their purchase, like so many secondhand double-deckers by Thames Valley, was to supplement the fleet at limited expense during a difficult period. As a result it was possible to dispose of AEC 'Regals' Nos.61/3-7 (MWL 878, NJO 217/8, OFC 204-6) during January.

From January 23rd the Maidenhead Coach Station was under water as part of extensive flooding in the town. The coach station had to be abandoned at 6pm as the waters reach that point, and in fact no through working was possible until the 28th. The weather subsequently turned much colder, leaving the coach station covered in three-quarters of an inch of ice, and it did not come back into use until 2nd February.

The coach station under water, with the main railway embankment behind.

The Irish Tour of 1958 had been very successful, but Leyland No.169 had returned to Newbury for Winter de-licensing afterwards, its place being taken for 1959 by pride-of-the-fleet Bristol MW6G No.803 (ORX 634).

The tours programme had been further developed for the 1959 season, with a number of combined tours being offered, listed as Tour Nos.10a-29 in the brochure. These put together pairs of existing SM tours, obviously aimed at those wishing to see as much of the Country as possible. A further clue to their main purpose may be discerned from the prices also being quoted in US dollars – indeed there were SM agents in both the US and Canada! For local passengers wishing to join the Cornwall and South Devon tours at Newbury, such an arrangement was made from 1959, partly to counter the expansion of the tours programme of Reliance of Newbury.

Further Bristol MW6G's with ECW C34F bodies were received in time for the new season, with Nos.804/ 7 (PRX 930/3) arriving in March, followed by 805/6 (PRX 931/2) during April.

Bristol MW coach No.805 (PRX 931) is seen picking up in Newbury Market Place on the South Devon tour not long after entering service.

The open-top double-decker emerged from hibernation in early June, first for use with the others at Epsom for The Derby, before taking up the sight-seeing duties at Oxford. It continued to carry a predominately cream livery, with only the mudguards and fleetname box in maroon. A repaint would have no doubt looked quite attractive, but it was to be make-or-break year for the open-toppers. The rest of the active fleet, barring perhaps a few of the 'Regals' earmarked for withdrawal, were all in the new livery by the end of June 1959

Above - SM was chosen to provide the official coach for the players of Oxford United FC for some years, and MW coach No.807 (PRX 933) was selected to serve in that role when seen on a misty morning at Gloucester Green. Below – Also at Gloucester Green, but over beyond the café where the SM coaches were usually to be found, was the repainted AEC 'Regal' IV under-floor engine coach N0.85 (SFC 571).

During 1959 the terminus for SM coaches in Worcester was moved from Newport Road Bus Station to the Croft Road Coach Station.

The weather in the Thames Valley area was very wet throughout the Summer of 1959, which again adversely affected operation of the open-topper. During September it was sent to join the others in store at Stokenchurch, pending a decision on their future. During October former N&D AEC 'Regal' coach No.68 (EJB 649) was sold, being followed by similar coaches Nos.56-9 (MJO 667, NFC 128-30) in November.

Despite having received the new livery, No.58 (NFC 129) was disposed of in 1959, though it certainly looked in good condition when seen at Victoria.

From January 1960 it was arranged that any TV booking office receiving bookings for SM tours could send them direct to Oxford, the practice being for them to go via HO since the take-over. Indeed, the tours business was very successful, with a further Ireland (Western Counties) holiday being added from 1960.

However, the pioneer Irish Tours coach No.169 (LWL 995) did not return there again, though it was re-licensed for use at Oxford up to its withdrawal at the end of July 1960. Prior to that in February, the last of the half-cab AEC 'Regals' had gone with the sale of ex-N&D No.70 (ERX 937). The 4 Guy coaches were withdrawn after Winter working and placed in store.

Former TV Bristol L6B No.552 (FMO 934) in maroon and cream livery seen in 1960 at the Iffley Road garage during the swan-song year of both.

Further transfers from the Thames Valley fleet were arranged to assist at Oxford, with Windover-bodied Bristol L6B No.552 (FMO 934) arriving in March, followed by similar Nos.545/51 (FMO 20/6) and 554/5 (FMO 936/7) in June. A pair of full-fronted ECW-bodied Bristol LWL6B's, Nos.608/9 (GBL 872/3) were also transferred in July 1960.

Only 1 year separated the delivery of the above L6B with this 1951 LWL6B with ECW 'Queen Mary' style coachwork, No.608, seen at Oxford.

143

New deliveries for 1960 consisted of a further quartet of Bristol MW6G's with C34F bodies by ECW. Nos.830-2 (UJB 196-8) were all received in March and No.833 (UJB 197) arrived during April.

Although the open-toppers were all re-licensed for The Derby again in early June 1960, both they and the Guy coaches were advertised for sale later that month. The Guys found a ready buyer in none other than Red & White, a fleet in which they looked very much at home! R&W even purchased one of the open-toppers, No.773 (CAP 211), albeit for use as a tree-lopper.

A later view of MW coach No.832 (UJB 198) during the period when some coaches were fitted with wheel trim both front and rear. In this 1964 view the coach is seen at TV's Lower Thorn Street premises, though its overhaul had just taken place at the Colonnade Works to the east of Reading.

Between 29th/30th August 1960 one of the MW6G's was made available to the British Transport Commission Film Unit for one of its regular films promoting coach travel, these films being shown as supplements to the main film and newsreels then standard fare for cinema-goers.

On 31st August Tom Pruett met with representatives of the Irish airline Aer Lingus, to discuss the possibility of altering the Western Counties tour for air access from the mainland, as it would seem that the reputation of the Irish Sea crossing was a deterrent to some would be customers.

The Oxford service van was No.27 (RWL 71), a 1953 Austin 10/12cwt, seen at Gloucester Green in September 1960, now surviving into preservation.

The end of season withdrawals in October saw the demise of Bristol L6B's Nos.550/2-4 (FMO 25, FMO 934-6), and the following month they were joined by mechanically-similar, but full-fronted, No.74 (EBD 237), all of which were disposed of. The Winter months were also a busy time when coaches received major overhauls and re-painting, whilst over the Winter of 1960/1 it was the turn of Bristol LS's 79-84 (SFC 565-70) to be up-seated to 39 for express and contract duties.

On Christmas Day 1960 TV operated no services whatsoever for the first time since its inception, though SM ran two journeys, one each on both the routes from London, leaving Victoria at 9am. Normal service resumed on Boxing Day and continued though TV crews were on strike on the 27th.

From 1st January 1961 Mr. Mitchell took the post of Depot Inspector at Oxford. From 9th of that month it was agreed that holders of Privilege Tickets at the Oxford and High Wycombe garages could make use of the SM express at one-quarter fare, but subject to seating being available.

Disposal of the Iffley Road garage was proposed, the first stage of which was to transfer it into TV ownership, which took place on 21st February. It was duly disposed of to the neighbouring City Motor Co. (Oxford) Ltd. for the sum of £21,500 on 16th June 1961, ending a link to the site since 1928.

Also during February 1961 agreement was made with the Ulster Transport Authority for the maintenance of the coach out-stationed for the revised tour of the Western & Northern Counties, which we will hear more of in due course. In order to operate in the UTA area, the coach would need to be technically transferred to its ownership. It should also be noted that PSV's operated in that region were still required to carry plates of a similar style to the old Hackney Carriage plates long discontinued on the mainland.

During March agreement was reached with Smith's Luxury Coaches (Reading) Ltd. to act as a booking agent for SM extended tours. For the 1961 season it was also decided that drivers would be issued with 2-piece suits in clerical grey. As usual, one of the tour coaches went on display at various points in the SM/TV area, but on 11th April it broke new ground by visiting Swindon, probably to counter expansion by Reliance of Newbury?

Back in February Bristol LS6B coach 693 (HMO 839) was returned to TV ownership. New vehicles on order consisted largely of more Bristol MW6G's with ECW C34F bodies. These arrived a little later than expected, with Nos.858/9 (WRX 773/4) being delivered in May, followed by No.860 (WRX 775) during June. May also saw the arrival of the first of a number of lightweight Bedford types for touring work, this being No.861 (WRX 776). It was a Leyland-engined SB8 type, but of 7ft 6ins width, and carried a Duple C37F body. The main role of this coach was the Wye Valley tours, on which it took the place of sold L6B No.74 (EBD 237).

The narrow 'Super Vega' bodied Bedford No.861 (WRX 776) is seen on a damp day, about to set off for the Wye Valley tour based at Symonds Yat.

For the 1961 season, the Company became involved in its first venture of coach-air travel, when the Ireland (Western Counties) tour was accessed via Bristol Airport. The quicker transit to Ireland also allowed the tour to be extended into the Northern Counties as well, this being a holiday of continual touring. An additional two-centre tour started that year was 8 days in North Wales, based at the Craigside Hotel, Llundudno and the Victoria Hotel at Llanberis.

Bristol MW No.858 (WRX 773) is seen on tour somewhere in Scotland. The combination of the SM fleetname integrated with the radiator grille and the ECW 'wings' provided a pleasing front end. In later years a number of these coaches received standard grilles without the fleetname panel as a result of accidental damage.

On 30th July one of the MW touring coaches was made available to London Coastal Coaches publicity people and posed for photos in Oxford, this being for inclusion of the 1962 tours programme in the next LCC brochure. In consideration of this additional publicity, SM duly agreed to pay LCC 9% of bookings received for that season.

Another bad smash involving a SM coach occurred at Ashridge Hill, near East Ilsley on 6th October at 7.30am. The coach was on a contract run when it was run into by a car-transporter, which was in the process of overtaking

147

The rear of Bristol LS6G No.84 (SFC 570) after the early morning smash.

another lorry. The rear end was extensively damaged and two of the coach passengers died as a result. The vehicle was beyond economical repair, being transferred to TV ownership on 23rd November and dismantled for spares.

Withdrawals of a scheduled nature during October were ex-UCOC fully-fronted LL6B's with 8ft wide bodywork Nos.821/6 (FRP 835/41), as well as the last 7ft 6ins wide former UCOC L6B No.73 (EDB 236). The latter had been used on one of the Wye Valley tours, being replaced by another Bedford of the same width in course of preparation for the following year.

During November 1961 the last of the Windover-bodied Bristol L6B's from the TV fleet was withdrawn. These stylish, but by then rather dated, coaches had been used extensively during their final season, all resplendent in the maroon and cream livery, No.551 (FMO 26) being the last to go. Two former TV Bristol LS coaches were transferred to SM in December 1961. No.673 (HBL 75) was an LS6G new in 1952, whilst No.688 (HMO 834) was an LS6B of the 1953 deliveries.

Another United Counties connection occurred during December, when that operator decided to end its extended tours, and discussions took place between the operators on how SM might assist in providing alternatives.

Chapter Nineteen   The Big Freeze

Windover-bodied Bristol L6B No.555 (FMO 937) shines in the sun during its days with SM. It is, however, seen on hire to TV at Reading, probably on Royal Ascot Race Week duties, when SM coaches were also drafted in.

The early '60's were an interesting period in terms of the vehicles in use, as the old half-cab types were still very much in evidence, alongside the under-floor engined types, which themselves started to give way to those with engines at the rear. Also of particular significance was the increase in the permitted dimensions of PSV's to a width of 8ft 2.5ins and maximum length of 36ft – which at the time seemed quite enormous!

At the time the regulations changed, there were two coaches on order from Bristol/ECW and destined for the TV/SM fleets. TV vehicle programme documents show that these were to have both been Bristol MW's when first ordered for 1962 delivery. Later one became listed as a 36-footer, but still as an MW, presumably pending Bristol's announcement of a designation. Although the MW did in fact get delivered as planned in April 1962, No.866 (520 ABL) was assigned to the TV fleet – though we shall note its later transfer to Oxford in due course. The 36-footer, duly designated REX (for Rear Engine eXperimental) was, however, delayed and did not appear until a year later, being the prototype of the high-floor version of the new chassis intended for coaching work and was allocated to the SM fleet.

Another bad smash affected the fleet on 10th February, when LS coach No.692 (HMO 838) was involved in a collision with a private car at Nuneham Courtenay. The car occupants died as a result and the coach was badly damaged, its place being taken by the re-licensing of LL6B No.77 (FRP 834).

Routine fleet changes saw Bristol LS6B No.691 (HMO837) transfer to SM during January 1962 in place of withdrawn LL6B 825 (FRP 840). In March further transfers from TV were Bristol LWL6B No.610 (GBL 874) and LS6G No.671 (HBL 73), resulting in the demise of LL6B's Nos.822/4/7 (FRP 837/9/42).

Bristol LWL coach No.610 (GBL 874) lays over in The Grange Car Park after being called upon to assist during Royal Ascot Race Week in 1962.

On 14th February 1962 the South Midland Agency Conference was hosted at the London Coastal Coaches offices at Victoria Coach Station, with booking agents invited to the event. Exhibitions, and even live entertainment, was provided by the Tourist Boards of Scotland, Wales, Northern Ireland and Eire, whilst 2 of the Company's coaches were put on display in the coach station. Changes to operations that season saw the end of the through coaches to Brighton, Eastbourne and Margate. The Northern Ireland tour became Donegal & Northern Ireland, whilst a new venture was a 6-day tour of East Anglia.

Deliveries of new coaches for 1962 were all Bedfords, with SB8-types 862-5 (516-9 ABL) all being licensed on 1st May. Prior to that date, as had been a tradition harking back to pre-war days at TV, arrangements were made to show one of the coaches off at various locations. This started with Maidenhead on 23rd February, followed by Reading from 8th March, Newbury from 15th March, Slough on 27th March and Swindon on 27th April.

Of the Bedfords, No.862 was the 7ft. 6ins replacement for LL6B No.73 on the Wye Valley tour, whilst the others were all 8-footers, all carrying 'Super Vega' coachwork by Duple of Hendon.

Bedford coach No.865 (519 ABL) on display outside the Travel Office in Reading Stations Square. Note the brochure pages placed in the windows. The application of the SM livery varied with different Duple body styles.

With the completion of the new Coventry Cathedral in May 1962, an excursion there was duly added, whilst on 27th September another long-serving employee departed with the retirement of Inspector A. Morgan.

As 1962 came to a close the usual round of heavy maintenance, repaints etc. got underway. November saw MW6G's Nos.803/4 (ORX 634 and PRX 930) re-seated to C38F for express duties, whilst the following month was marked by the withdrawal of ex-UCOC LL6B No.75 (FRP 832). January 1963 saw MW's 801/2 (ORX 632/3) up-seated to C38F, whilst similar coaches 805-7 (PRX 931-3) had been similarly treated by March.

Bristol LWL6B No.610 (GBL 874) shown on hire to City of Oxford during the big freeze of 1962-3. Note the makeshift destination board in the nearside front window and the damage to the front bumper–there were few vehicles in the fleet without a knock or two before the freeze had ended!

As anyone who was around in those days will readily recall, the Winter of 1962/3 produced one of the longest periods of freezing weather in modern history. Although some might argue that the 1947 freeze was worse, that was over sooner, as it was early March before some normality returned.

The problems of operating express services through largely rural areas is all too obvious, whilst much of the regular contract work necessitated the use of even more rural stretches, isolated villages and runs over the Berkshire Downs in particular. However, one of the greatest challenges came not from within its own operations, difficult enough though they were, but from the neighbouring City of Oxford Motor Services. The latter fleet soon suffered from accident damage, combined with a shortage of maintenance staff, with the result that it proved necessary to hire in vehicles from other operators. As it was, TV had drafted a pair of LS coaches to Reading to cover for accident victims from 19th February, though of course a sizeable portion of the SM fleet was de-licensed over the Winter each year.

SM made available a number of vehicles to COMS for the purpose on a daily basis, a summary of which is shown on the following page.

Dates	Coaches	Dates	Coaches
22.1.63	81, 85, 610	12/4.2.63	673
23.1.63	81, 85, 93	18.2.63	671
24.1.63	81, 93, 610	19.2.63	671, 673
25.1.63	80, 81, 610	21.2.63	608, 673
26.1.63	79, 80, 610	22/3.2.63	82, 671, 673, 688
28/9.1.63	81, 83, 610	25-8.2.63	82, 671, 673, 688
31.1.63	610	1-3.3.63	82, 671, 673, 688
1.2.63	76	4.3.63	82, 673, 688
5-8.2.63	608	5.3.63	79, 671, 673, 688
11/3/5.2.63	80	6-8.3.63	79, 671, 688

Note: All of the above were Bristol LS's, except for No.85 (AEC 'Regal' IV) and Nos.608/10 (Bristol LWL's), all fitted with ECW bodies.

The first of the new coaches for 1963 arrived in February as No.C401, TV having devised a fleet numbering scheme separating double-deckers, single-deckers and coaches in series commencing D1, S301 and C401. It was a Bedford SB8 with Duple 'Bella Vega' C37F body and registered as 831 CRX. It was soon sent on a publicity tour throughout February, starting at Burnham on 5th, Slough on 8th, Maidenhead on 15th and High Wycombe on 28th. In the light of experience for touring work, these were fitted with a 45-gallon fuel tank, whilst the previous Bedfords had only 26-gallon tanks.

Bedford C403 (833 CRX) on a tour of Scotland in its original livery. It was duly decided to add more cream paint after their first season.

153

Former UCOC Bristol LL6B coach No.78 (FRP 836) was withdrawn in March 1963, whilst similar coaches Nos.76 (FRP 833), 823 (FRP 838) and 77 (FRP 834) were weeded out during May, July and August respectively, thereby eliminating that batch entirely from the fleet.

The remaining pair of Bedfords were delivered as C402/3 (832/3 CRX) in April and both carried Duple 'Bella Vega' C37F bodies for touring work. However the big news was the receipt, on 25th April, of the long-awaited Bristol REX6G No.867, which kept its pre-booked registration 521 ABL.

No.867 shortly after being received, emerging from The Colonnade Works in Reading, a building originally constructed to house the Thackray's Way fleet of Gilford coaches. The prototype ECW body incorporated fixed side windows and forced-air ventilation, whilst the front end had been developed from the 'new look' MW of 1962, but with a more modern FLF-style radiator grille. The stepped waistrail slightly spoilt the overall look and was eliminated on production models. The fog lamps also proved very vulnerable to accidental damage and were repositioned higher in due course. Note also the wheel trims, though the front ones didn't last long.

The REX was intended for evaluation mainly on the express routes, though it also had a number of visits back to Bristol Commercial Vehicles in its first year as various modifications were instigated in the light of the benefit of operational experience.

Above - Duple-bodied Bedford SB8 No.864 (518 ABL) is seen on the Mid Wales tour at Llandrindod Wells during the 1962 season. The use of Bedford chassis for touring purposes occurred in a number of BTC fleets, largely due to their being no lightweight Bristol chassis available. Another factor was the waiting time for ECW bodies, which duly resulted in the search for alternatives. Below - The next batch of Duple-bodied Bedford SB8's included C401 (831 CRX), which is shown at Oxford after the additional cream paint was added to the side panels and the radiator grille surround, which considerably 'lightened' their general appearance.

An interesting meeting took place in early April between the Area Traffic Manager and the Head Postmaster of Oxford, to discuss the possibility of hiring laid-up SM coaches as a means of coping with the Christmas postal peak, and it was agreed to implement the arrangement for the 1963 period.

Other meetings also took place concerning the future parking place for coaches out-stationed in London, as the arrangement to use the London Transport Victoria (Gillingham Street) depot came to an end on 16th May.

The Scotland tour had proven very popular indeed, so two versions were made available, one of 9-day duration and the other at 11 days. The tour of Donegal and Northern Ireland was re-named Donegal & the Ulster Coast and amended to 10 days, but without the benefit of air transfer from 1963. The East Anglia tour had not received much interest and was dropped.

For the 1963 season Bedford SB8 No.863 (517 ABL) covered the Southern Ireland tour, being seen awaiting its passengers arrival at the quay side.

For the Summer of 1963 all the SM express routes were given route letters which continued the series used by Thames Valley's London expresses A and B. For obvious reasons, this once again raised the possibility that SM would loose its separate identity. In fact no such motive was behind the move, and there was even an alternative rumour that the A and B would be transferred to SM operation, but that was equally unfounded!

No. 82 (SFC 568) was one of the initial batch of Bristol LS's, seen here in its final form with maroon and cream livery, fleetname boxes, fixed front windows and flashing trafficators. It awaits departure from the Gloucester Green coach stand on one of the faster London-bound journeys.

The SM services were allocated route letters as follows:-
Route C Oxford – Henley – Maidenhead – London
Route D Oxford – High Wycombe – Uxbridge – London
Route E Worcester – Oxford – Maidenhead – London
Route F Worcester – Oxford – Newbury – Winchester – Southsea
At the same time, TV's own seasonal expresses were also brought into the same series as:-
Route G High Wycombe – Maidenhead – Southsea
Route H High Wycombe – Bournemouth
Route J High Wycombe – Eastbourne - Hastings

During July yet another transfer from the TV fleet arrived at Oxford, in the shape of 1952 Bristol LS6G with ECW C39F body No.674 (HBL 76). No further alterations to the fleet took place throughout the Summer.

Some of the journeys on Route D were operated as non-stop between Headington (Nr. Oxford) and Kensington (London), which reduced the journey time from 2hrs 44mins to 2hrs 15mins. These arrangements came in from the onset of the Winter timetable on 1st November 1963. Also from that date the 5-minute layover at Maidenhead was discontinued.

Between December 1963 and January 1964 a number of older SM coaches, including LS's Nos.83 and 671 (SFC 569 and HBL 73) a MW's Nos.805, 807 and 830 (PRX 931/3 and UJB 196) received 'C' prefixes to their fleet numbers in error.

As previously noted, there had been a meeting between SM and the Post Office regarding the possible use of spare coaches to assist in handling the large volume of Christmas post. Between 16th-24th December 1963 4 coaches were so used, having been stripped of their seats, with the exception of a pair of seats immediately behind the driver, the rest of the space being piled high with mailbags. TV were paid £227 10s 3d for the use of the quartet, and whole exercise was deemed a success. Once again no services were operated on TV routes on Christmas, but the customary SM journeys from London to Oxford departed on both routes at 9am for those wishing to leave the capital.

During November LS6B coaches Nos.689-91 (HMO 835-7) were taken out of service for conversion to service saloons for further use by TV on the new Route 19 (Reading – Long Lane) operated jointly with Reading CT.

Coaches on the Southsea express made a comfort stop at the municipal coach station on the outskirts of Winchester, from where MW No.860 (WRX 775) will take the by-pass in order to avoid the ancient city centre.

Chapter Twenty   Motorway Ahead

From 1st January 1964 Oxford had a new Garage Foreman, in the shape of Mr. J. Sanders. Deliveries of new coaches also got underway that month, which was a relief considering the pressure SM's regular suppliers were under at the time. Indeed, the situation at ECW was so severe that they had to announce that no coaches would be constructed for 1965, in order that the backlog of orders for bus bodies could be met!

During January a pair of production Bristol RELH6G's were received as Nos.C404/5 (834/5 CRX). These were the development of the REX, but now designated as <u>RE</u> <u>L</u>ong-wheelbase <u>H</u>igh floor, and both carried C47F bodies by ECW.

C404 (834 CRX) not long after entry into service. The appearance of the body was very similar to the prototype, but the slightly awkward-looking stepped waistrail was eliminated. These coaches gave a good ride and were excellent work-horses on the express routes and occasional excursion runs.

The remaining new vehicles for 1964, also delivered in January, were three Bedford SB13's for touring work. Nos.C407-9 (837/8/42 CRX) carried 37-seater Duple 'Super Vega' bodywork. Once again, the Bedfords were fitted with 45-gallon fuel tanks, whereas the Bristol RE's only had 34-gallon tanks. Whilst the Bedfords only weighed 5tons 6qtrs 2cwt, the RE's were 8tons 5qtrs 2cwt, though the latter were actually 1cwt less than the under-floor engined 30ft long Guys delivered some 21 years previously!

Bedford SB13 No.C408 (838 CRX) is seen on Watlington Hill. Note the variations in livery with the previous batch, each style of Duple body calling for a different interpretation.

From 19th February 1964 the license for operating the Oxford café was put with Coach Caterers (Southern) Ltd., ending 31 years of direct involvement in running the refreshments at that location.

For the 1964 season tours drivers once again had a change of wardrobe, with the issue of black blazers and dark grey trousers. That year's Northern Ireland coach was MW No.804 (PRX 930), which was fitted with NI Plate No.3158 for that purpose. For the convenience of passengers wishing to join SM tours at Oxford, an 8am journey from London via High Wycombe was put on from 11th May.

Tours for 1964 were substantially as before, though the Wye Valley tour was dropped – as this was one of the first SM tours, it can only be assumed that everyone who wanted to go had already been! The Scotland tours were slightly re-organised to operate as 9 and 12-days versions.

With the new coaches safely delivered, the withdrawal took place in April of Bristol LWL6B's Nos.608/10 (GBL 872/4), followed by similar vehicle No.609 (GBL 873) the following month. This finally eliminated front-engined Bristols from the fleet of once-numerous varieties of L, LL and LWL types in both half-cab and full-fronted forms.

The Tilling Association Film Unit once again asked TV/SM to assist in the making of a promotional film for coach touring holidays. On 22nd May 1964 TV's 'new look' MW No.866 (520 ABL) and the REX No. 867 (521 ABL) were made available for filming in the country north of Basingstoke. 867 was used again on 12th June, when filming took place near Basingstoke and Maidenhead, as well as when static in Lower Thorn Street, Reading.

A rear end comparison of the REX prototype No.867 and one of the 1964 pair of RELH's, seen on their regular bay at Victoria Coach Station.

Overnight parking arrangements at Worcester were further revised from 19th August, when the coaches were transferred from Croft Road Coach Station to the Midland Red garage in Padmore Street.

As previously noted, Eastern Coach Works could not supply coaches for 1965 delivery, leading to the decision to order from Harrington instead! In fact TV had taken bodies from that builder back in 1939, most of which had ended their days on SM reliefs in 1954, whilst SM itself had also favoured that supplier during the '30's. These 3 coaches were in fact received in record time, actually arriving in August 1964, but they were placed in store until the following year!

On 18th October the 24-hour clock was adopted for use in all SM timetables, whilst the last day of that month saw the introduction of some journeys on Route C making use of the completed section of the M4 motorway, but of course omitting Maidenhead and Slough. Whilst using the motorway undoubtably provided faster journeys for through passengers, the SM express routes had always benefited from good patronage at places served along the way, so in hindsight it is possible to see that the increased use of motorways actually alienated many potential passengers. At the time though, passengers from Maidenhead and Slough still had the TV service B for limited stop journeys to London.

During August, one-time show coach No.803 (ORX 634) had lost its nearside air-horn to a tree at Woburn Park. It ran in that form until December when the other one was removed. Accidental damage was also behind the decision to relocate the fog lamps on RE's C404/5 to front bumper level during November, with No.867 receiving the same treatment in December.

Motorway travel also exposed the need to replace the winding windscreens on the 1952 Bristol LS's with fixed units, as they tended to 'whistle' at high speed! Nos.79 and 80 were dealt with in December 1964, and the rest of that year's deliveries were done over the Winter months. The conversion of LS's into saloon buses for the Thames Valley fleet was also further extended with the treatment of No.688 (HMO 834) in October, followed by No.692 (HMO 838) during December.

Bedford SB13 coach No.C407 (837 CRX) takes a break at the Winchester Coach Station and café before continuing its day tour. One advantage of these types of bodywork was the popular seats to the left of the driver.

The Bristol MW6G's were sound work-horses throughout the late '50's and the '60's, but like all of the fleet at that time they were invariably kept in good condition. No.831 (UJB 197) gleams at Botley Road in June 1964.

Once again SM loaned a quartet of stripped out coaches to the Oxford P.O. for the busy Christmas period, with Bristol LS's 81/2 (SFC 567/8) and 692/3 (HMO 838/9) serving on this occasion. Of the latter pair, 693 had actually returned to TV ownership in 1961, but had previously been with SM, whilst 692 had just come to the end of its Oxford days, as both were for conversion to service saloons. Indeed, work had already started on 693, so it ran in coach livery, but with a jacknife door, bus indicator at front and fluorescent lighting fitted! The exercise brought in £212 4s 3d.

The tours programme for 1965 had a 5-day tour of West Wales added, which lasted for one season only. The full list, complete with the weekly cost of all accommodation, meals, day tours and any associated entrance fees was as below:-

Tour Name	Days	Base	Cost £ s d
Scotland	12	Touring	£47 15 00
Scotland	9	Loch Long Hotel, Arrochar	£35 00 00
Southern Ireland	10	Touring	£42 00 00
Donegal & Ulster Coast	9	Touring	£38 15 00
English Lakes	8	Grand Hotel, Grange-over-Sands	£32 00 00
Cornwall	8	Bay Hotel, Newquay	£30 10 00

Welsh Coast	8	Seabank Hotel, Porthcawl	£29 10 00
North Wales	8	Craigside Hotel, Llandudno and	
		Victoria Hotel, Llanberis	£29 15 00
Mid Wales	8	Glen Usk Hotel, Llandrindod Wells	£23 15 00*
North Devon	8	Dilkusha Grand Hotel, Ilfracombe	£27 15 00
South Devon	8	Abbey Lawn Hotel, Torquay	£24 15 00*
West Wales	5	Castle Malgwyn Hotel, Llechryd	£20 15 00

weekly price variable according to quality of hotel room on these tours

The outstationing of coaches in London still needed a longer-term solution, though Samuelsons were looking after them *inter alia* at their premises opposite Victoria Coach Station. During February there was talk of using LT premises at Camberwell, but during early March a deal was concluded to use LT's Walworth garage instead. Also during February, the ownership of all SM vehicles, plant, machinery and fixtures and fittings passed to TV.

March saw the licensing of the trio of Bedfords with Harrington 'Crusader' IV bodies as C410-2 (EMO 551-3C). These were 37-seaters, mainly for use on tours.

Harrington-bodied C412 is seen when new on a Scottish tour. This batch had more cream paint than the contemporary Duple bodies, making them appear both lighter and taller.

The Harrington-bodied Bedfords were also used on excursions at times.
No.C410 (EMO 551C) ventured to Southsea on a sunny day in 1965. These
were particularly comfortable coaches to travel on, though they lacked the
roof quarter-lights usually associated with SM touring stock.

As a result of the new arrivals, Bedford SB8-types Nos. 862/3 (516/7 ABL) were transferred to the TV fleet, the former being a 7ft 6ins example, both departing during April. In that same month another former TV Bristol LS6G with ECW C39F body No.672 (HBL 74) transferred to the SM fleet. During the early Spring MW6G coaches Nos.830-3 (UJB 196-9) were re-seated to C38F for express work. For that season the coaches for the tours of Ireland were C401 (which carried Northern Plate No.3128) and C402, the latter covering the tours in the Republic. Further evidence of the demotion of the remaining 1961/2 Bedfords Nos.861 (WRX 776) and 864/5 (518/9 ABL) came when the 'extended tours' lettering on their rear panels was painted over during 1965.

During August 1965 extensive remodelling took place of the Maidenhead Bus Station, which resulted in the Coach Station being turned over to the bus routes. Coaches made use of the available areas of the Bus Station until 19th November. From 30th September a further staff benefit was agreed, when Newbusy-based holders of privilege tickets were permitted to use them on the popular Oxford - Southsea express route.

End of season withdrawals in September resulted in the demise of Bristol LS's Nos.79-83 (SFC 565-9), all of which were disposed of as their front windscreen arrangement rendered them unsuitable for conversion to service saloons. The same was true of No.673 (HBL 75), which left the fleet in October. However, the batch including Nos.90/1 (TWL 55/6) were suitable and work commenced on them during October and November respectively.

As noted previously, fairly frequent modifications took place on the RE's during their earlier years, with the rear suspension system on 867 and C404/5 being dealt with in December 1965.

Also during December there was a new addition to the fleet, though a non-PSV in this case. Austin van No.27 (RWL 71) was replaced by No.ED59 (GJB 227C), an Austin 'Gypsy'. The prefix 'ED' stood for Engineering Department and had been introduced by TV at the same time that new PSV's were divided into D, S and C-series.

4 coaches were again loaned to the Oxford Postmaster in the period 17-24th December, though their identities were not recorded, bringing in an income of £114 9s 0d – rates seemingly having much reduced since previous years.

The 'Gypsy' was the Austin equivalent to the Land Rover, and SM's was nicely turned out in fleet livery, flashing emergency light and front winch.

Chapter Twenty One   Groovin' Along

From 1st January 1966 the 23.00 London – High Wycombe – Oxford route was amended to set down passengers at all bus stops between 'Wycombe and Stokenchurch, which added a further 7 minutes to the running time.

On 1st February a meeting took place with representatives of Bristol Omnibus Co. Ltd. to discuss how SM and the Greyhound routes might work together in light of the latter's desire to make more use of the growing motorway network. This resulted in passengers on the Greyhound coaches from 24th May for intermediate points between Oxford and London, and on routes from Weston-super-Mare, Devizes and Swindon, would change onto SM coaches at Oxford. From 15th October this also applied to services from Bristol, Bath and Faringdon, as the pioneering operator deserted some of its longest-established roads in favour of the motorways.

For the 1966 season Duple-bodied Bedford VAM14 coaches were ordered. No.C415 (GRX 415D) is seen covering the South Devon tour in the Torbay area on a glorious day.

A quartet of Bedford coaches had been ordered for 1966 delivery, though the first pair, Nos.C413/4 (GRX 413/4D) were actually received in the last month of 1965, going straight into storage. The remaining pair, Nos.C415/6 (GRX 415/6D) followed in March and all were licensed from 1st April. In anticipation of this move, a further trio of Bristol LS's had been earmarked

The Bedford VAM's were equally at home on the express services, as they possessed a true front entrance. No.C416 (GRX 416D) is seen at the long-established Gloucester Green coach stands, adjacent to the handy café.

for conversion to service saloons, with Nos.92/3 (TWL 57/8) departing in February, followed by No.95 (TWL 60) during April. All surviving older coaches were fitted with rear flashing trafficators during early 1966.

As already noted several times, various events in connection with livery changes and ownership of vehicles, had led to speculation that SM might be absorbed into the parent Thames Valley. The 1965 South Midland tours block used in various publications had actually included details of TV's A and B routes between Reading and London, but without any mention that they were not SM operations. Imagine then the local speculation when the Bristol FLF double-decker coaches used on those routes started appearing in the maroon and cream livery – albeit with TV fleetnames! In fact, they all carried an offside staircase panel advert for South Midland tours.

As regards TV's other coaching activities at Reading, a chronic shortage of drivers caused that Company to cease all advertised excursion work from 20th June 1966. As a result of this, the 1962 Bristol MW6G with ECW C39F body, No.866 (520 ABL) was transferred to operate 'on hire' to SM.

An interesting exchange of vehicles took place between 1st August and 1st September, whereby Bedford VAM No.C416 was loaned to Timpsons in place of Duple-bodied AEC 'Reliance' registered JJD 568D, each operator making comparison of their respective performance.

During November 1966 two Bristol LS coaches were withdrawn, these being Nos.672/4 (HBL 74/6), though another of that original TV batch, No.675 (HBL 77) was transferred to Oxford the following month. During December another LS, No.94 (TWL 59) was withdrawn for conversion to a service saloon. Also that month MW No.866 left Oxford, probably for store at The Colonnade Works in Reading, having been a useful addition at Oxford during that Summer.

Bristol MW No.866 (520 ABL) seen at Victoria Coach Station during its 6 month stint working for SM. Note the 'on hire' sticker in the offside indicator box. This carried the 'new look' ECW body of 1962, and was the only example to come to the TV/SM fleets, though the design was obviously developed for the REX, including the stepped waistrail.

For the pre-Christmas period a similar number of coaches were hired to the Oxford GPO, including former No.95 (TWL 60) which was undergoing its metamorphosis to become Thames Valley No.S320. These conversions were by no means unique to the TV examples, as a number of other BTC fleets sought to make continued use of coaches that were being replaced.

169

Above- Bristol RELH6G No.C423 (LJB 423E) at the re-designed Maidenhead Bus Station on the route to Worcester. Below- C422 (LJB 422E) at Oxford on the C route to London via Maidenhead. Note the larger destination screens and the jacknife doors, whilst internally these coaches differed from previous examples in having a driver's cage and semi-automatic gears. These coaches were delivered with fog lamps raised out of harms way, in the same place where those on Nos.867 and C404/5 had their lamps relocated after being prone to accidental damage.

A trio of Bristol RELH6G coaches formed the new deliveries for 1967 with No.C421 (LJB 421E) arriving in April, followed by Nos.C422/3 (LJB 422/3E) in May. During April Bristol MW's 858-60 (WRX 773-5) received chrome wheel discs on both front and rear wheels similar to those fitted to the RE's. Meanwhile, the stint in the Republic of Ireland for the 1967 season fell to Bedford VAM14 No.C416 (GRX 416D), but otherwise the year was a quiet one for fleet changes.

Despite various new deliveries over the years, the older units of the fleet were nonetheless active. 1952 Bristol LS6G No.675 (HBL 77) originated in the TV fleet, ending its days on SM contract work. However, as this 1967 view shows, it was maintained in excellent condition to the end.

Bristol LS No.675 (HBL 77) was withdrawn in August 1967, followed by the last of the type in use, No.671 (HBL 73), during October. Also during October the AEC 'Regal' IV No.85 (SFC 571) was withdrawn, remarkably it had actually outlasted the standard Bristol LS's new to SM at the same time – not bad for an 'oddity' only reluctantly accepted by the new owners!

For the 1967 tours programme, an new 9-day Isle of Man tour was added, with a base at the Grand Island Hotel in Ramsey. On the South Devon tour the venue was changed to the Lincombe Hall Hotel, Torquay, whilst that used for the Mid Wales tour was re-located at the Commodore Hotel in Llandrindod Wells. The tours then entered a settled phase, with none added or deleted for the following two years.

1968 saw COMS with another vehicle shortage, as that bus company could not compete with the wages on offer at Oxford's motor factories and other industries. SM once again helped out, with peak-time loans as required:-

Dates	Coaches	Dates	Coaches
1.11.68	833, 858	6.11.68	832, 833, 858, C411
4.11.68	831, 833, 858, C409	7.11.68	831, 833, 858
5.11.68	831, 833, 858, C411	8.11.68	831, 832, 833, 858

Note - 831-3, 858 were ECW-bodied Bristol MW6G's, C409 was a Duple-bodied Bedford SB8 and C411 a Harrington-bodied Bedford SB13.

A pair of the original coaches used for the Reading – Heathrow Rail Air Link service were demoted in May 1968 and transferred to the SM fleet. No.C417 (LJB 417E) is seen at Gloucester Green. Note the old school building behind the coach, and also girl in the mini-dress worn to the left!

Amongst the vehicles added in May 1968 were two Bedford VAM14's with Duple 'Viceroy' C41F bodies, formerly based at Reading. Nos.C417/8 (LJB 417/8E) were new in January 1967.

New deliveries of coaches also entered service in May 1968, in the shape of Bristol LH6L's Nos.C428-31 (RJB 428-31F), all of which carried Duple 'Commander III' C41F bodies. As a result of these deliveries, Bedford SB8 Nos.864/5 (518/9 ABL) were withdrawn in May and June respectively. In October 1968 newer SB8's Nos.C401-3 (831-3 CRX) were also withdrawn. The other withdrawals that year took place in December, when Bristol MW coaches Nos.800/3 (ORX 631/4) were earmarked for conversion to buses.

Above - One of the two MW's selected for conversion was 800 (ORX 631), then 10 years old. As with the LS conversions, this involved the building up of the front dome for bus indicators, the fitting of a jacknife door and fluorescent saloon lighting. The cantrail windows were, however retained, making them pleasant vehicles for a ride through the Thames Valley countryside! Below – The Bristol LH, a lightweight model with underfloor engine and using mainly ready made parts, provided an alternative to the succession of Bedford types. No.C429 (RJB 429F) prepares to leave on an excursion from Oxford on a fine day in 1968. Note the size of the windows on the side and the lack of depth to the front windscreen.

The Bristol LH's had Leyland engines, as indeed had SM's Bedford SB8 and SB13 types delivered in the period 1961-7. No.C431 (RJB 431F) is about to leave Oxford for London, these coaches being used widely on both touring work and express services.

1968 was a significant year for the bus industry, as the Transport Holding Company (successor to the BTC) acquired the bus interests of the BET Group. This not only placed the bulk of the larger operating companies in State hands, but it meant that both SM and its old rival City of Oxford were at last in the same camp!

It was doubtless inevitable that the THC would review the operating areas of its constituent companies, as most area agreements between the old Tilling Group and BET concerns dated back to the early '20's. To facilitate this process, the Transport Act 1968 set up the National Bus Company to take over the various bus companies, with effect on 1st January 1969.

The South Midland fleet-name, but for how much longer would it be in use?

Chapter Twenty Two   The Name Lives On

Back in October 1967 SM had disposed of its last Bristol LS coach, whilst more recently it had started to lose the earlier MW's for conversion to TV service buses. Indeed, two further examples, Nos.801/2 (ORX 632/3) were selected during March 1969.

It therefore came as quite a surprise to find SM acquiring a trio of Bristols from Eastern National, two being very late LS's and the third an early MW also during March!

Two of the ex-ENOC coaches were Bristol LS6G's with ECW C34F bodies incorporating cantrail windows and extra windows in the front dome and twin destination indicators built into the front panel. The extra waistrail beading had been added later by ENOC and the green plastic inserts were retained during the repaint into SM colours, as was the cream and light green interior finish. No.440 (613 JPU) is seen at Oxford in June 1969.

The LS's were Nos.C432/3 (613/4 JPU) and were new in March 1957, whilst the MW6G had been new in January 1958 and became No.C434 (618 JPU). 613 JPU of the LS's had run under the ENOC subsidary fleetname Westcliff-on-Sea when new. However, it was soon realised that the fleet numbers allocated had already been notified to Duple Motor Bodies in respect of new coaches in course of completion, so the trio were re-numbered as 440-2 in April 1969, the practice of using the C prefix then being discontinued. They were in excellent condition and a good purchase.

Above – The other of the 2 LS's from Eastern National was 441 (614 JPU), seen on the bus stands at Gloucester Green. In common with SM, their original owner had operated a programme of extended tours and kept its coaches in exceptional condition. The style of body differs in many details with SM's own 1952-4 examples, being the final stage in the evolution of the first design of body used for the replacement MW chassis. Below – The MW became 442 (618 JPU) and differed only in detail externally from the LS's, most notable of which was the provision of a radiator grille in the front panel. It is seen at Southsea having worked the express route there.

A number of the remaining MW's, including No.858 (WRX 773) were up-seated during their Spring preparation to C38F for express duties, as had been the custom for many years. The former Rail Air Bedford VAM's Nos.C417/8 were in use extensively throughout the Summer, though they were not only at Oxford, being seen back at Reading from time to time. Indeed, the TV MW No.866 had become a spare vehicle for the Rail Air route after it had left SM, being fitted with a two-way radio for that duty.

New coaches for 1969 entered service in May in the shape of 432-5 (UMO 688-91G), all being Bristol LH6L's with Duple 'Commander IV' bodies seating 41.

The bodies on the 1969 LH's incorporated more bright-work on the sides, which affected the balance between the cream and maroon paintwork, leading to an overall darker appearance. No.433 (UMO 689G) is seen in George Street, Bath on a break in the journey on the North Devon tour.

No changes took place to the tours programme for 1969, but the office at 118 High Street, Oxford was disposed on 1st September, with all bookings being concentrated on the Gloucester Green Enquiry Office.

Bristol MW No.807 (PRX 933) was the next to go for conversion to a bus in August 1969, followed by Nos.804/5 (PRX 930/1) in October, then 806

Part of the interior of Botley Road garage in 1969. At each end of the line up are Bristol MW's, with No.833 (UJB 199) at the rear and No.859 (WRX 774) towards the entrance, both of which now sport standard issue grilles as the result of accidents. Between them are both the ex-ENOC LS's and No.C411 (EMO 552C) of the Harrington-bodied Bedford SB13's of 1965.

(PRX 932) during December. These conversions varied in the time taken to complete them, it being something of a 'spare-time' activity amongst the other maintenance necessities of the time! However, there was evidently an overall plan, as their new fleet numbers reflected the original sequence when new, but it was still interesting to speculate which emerged next!

September 1969 saw former Rail Air Bedford VAM No.C418 (LJB 418E) returning to TV ownership, whilst similar vehicle C417 (LJB 417E) was de-licensed for the Winter but returned to service at Oxford in Spring 1970.

During January 1970 City of Oxford experienced another of its periodic crises that left it with insufficient vehicles. South Midland once again stepped in with loaned coaches, with Bristol MW's Nos.833 (UJB 199) and 858 (WRX 773), together with the trio of Harrington-bodied Bedfords C410-2 (EMO 551-3C) serving that purpose between 19th-22nd January.

As part of movements to re-align operations of the National Bus Company, South Midland ceased to trade as a Company from 1st January 1970, all the

178

coaches already being in TV ownership for some time. Transfer of Botley Road garage to TV ownership also got underway, but was not completed until December of that year.

On 23rd February Bedford No.C411 (EMO 552C) was badly damaged in a collision with a Mercedes car, so SM hired Plaxton-bodied Ford F226-type MBW 199E from local independent Worth's Motor Services of Enstone.

Another quartet of Duple 'Commander IV'-bodied Bristol LH6L's were on order for 1970 delivery, but their arrival was slightly delayed. The first pair, Nos.436/7 (YBL 925/6H) were received as planned in May, but No.438 (YBL 927H) arrived in July, whilst No.439 (YBL 928H) was not available until September!

Bristol LH6L No.436 all shiny and new at Gloucester Green, one of the final batch of coaches delivered to South Midland Motor Services Ltd.

From 6th June the new Newlands Bus Station at High Wycombe came into use, with SM coaches also calling there. The bus station was adjacent to the new shopping precinct but, apart from being under cover, there was little to commend it in terms of passenger comfort. Finished in un-rendered concrete, the area was dull and soon became dirty, whilst the logic of the travelling public sharing its space with an open-plan bus garage only served to highlight the decline in standards and attitude in the industry and planners since the earlier days of this story.

On 17th July 1970 TV Rail Air Bristol RELH coach No.C424 (RJB 424F) caught fire on the M4 motorway near Littlewick Green, being badly damaged. As a result SM Bedford SB13 No.C408 (838 CRX) was taken by TV as a replacement, even though former Rail Air Bedford VAM No.C417 (LJB 417E) remained in SM service until November 1970! Bedford SB13 No.C407 (837 CRX) ended its SM days in September, whilst C409 (842 CRX) was also withdrawn in the Autumn. Also in September the first of the next batch of MW's, No.830 (UJB 196) went for conversion to a bus.

One apparent vehicular acquisition caused quite a stir during July and August 1970, when Royal Blue Bristol LS coach No.2203 (VDV 746) was standing in TV's Lower Thorn Street yard. Its arrival preceded C424's fire by a week, so a rumour it was a hasty replacement for the latter was clearly unfounded. However, the possibility that it might go to SM was not so far fetched, as it was one of the last of the type built and therefore no less likely than the 3 coaches recently acquired from Eastern National! As time went by, the alternative rumour that it was the first of 12 for conversion to service saloons was also circulating, whereas in fact the truth was rather more mundane, as it transpired that dealers had left it temporarily there in order to take other vehicles on – though at that time anything could turn up!

Still going strong was No.403 (521 ABL), the Bristol REX6G prototype, which had been No.867 until July 1969. Although it survived the next phase of South Midland ownership, sadly it did not make it into the realms of preserved vehicles, where it would have had considerable historical value.

However, the real news of 1970 was the merger with COMS, due to take place on 1st January 1971! Even when South Midland was considering selling out in the 1930's, COMS apparently took no interest. The new Company was to be known as Oxford-South Midland and the livery was to be maroon and cream, so elements of the old operator remained apparent. Transfer of ownership passed from the TV headquarters at Lower Thorn Street to the COMS base at 395 Cowley Road, Oxford, 33 coaches being transferred from SM as follows:-

No.	Reg. No.	Chassis	Bodywork	New	Acq.
831	UJB 197	Bristol MW6G	ECW C38F	3/60	New
832	UJB 198	Bristol MW6G	ECW C38F	3/60	New
833	UJB 199	Bristol MW6G	ECW C38F	4/60	New
858	WRX 773	Bristol MW6G	ECW C38F	5/61	New
859	WRX 774	Bristol MW6G	ECW C38F	5/61	New
860	WRX 775	Bristol MW6G	ECW C38F	6/61	New
403	521 ABL	Bristol REX6G	ECW C47F	4/63	New
404	834 CRX	Bristol RELH6G	ECW C47F	1/64	New
405	835 CRX	Bristol RELH6G	ECW C47F	1/64	New
410	EMO 551C	Bedford SB13	Harrington C37F	3/65	New
411	EMO 552C	Bedford SB13	Harrington C37F	3/65	New
412	EMO 553C	Bedford SB13	Harrington C37F	3/65	New
413	GRX 413D	Bedford VAM14	Duple C41F	12/65	New
414	GRX 414D	Bedford VAM14	Duple C41F	12/65	New
415	GRX 415D	Bedford VAM14	Duple C41F	3/66	New
416	GRX 416D	Bedford VAM14	Duple C41F	3/66	New
421	LJB 421E	Bristol RELH6G	ECW C47F	4/67	New
422	LJB 422E	Bristol RELH6G	ECW C47F	5/67	New
423	LJB 423E	Bristol RELH6G	ECW C47F	5/67	New
428	RJB 428F	Bristol LH6L	Duple C41F	5/68	New
429	RJB 429F	Bristol LH6L	Duple C41F	5/68	New
430	RJB 430F	Bristol LH6L	Duple C41F	5/68	New
431	RJB 431F	Bristol LH6L	Duple C41F	5/68	New
440	613 JPU	Bristol LS6G	ECW C34F	3/57	3/69
441	614 JPU	Bristol LS6G	ECW C34F	3/57	3/69
442	618 JPU	Bristol MW6G	ECW C34F	1/58	3/69
432	UMO 688G	Bristol LH6L	Duple C41F	5/69	New
433	UMO 689G	Bristol LH6L	Duple C41F	5/69	New
434	UMO 690G	Bristol LH6L	Duple C41F	5/69	New
435	UMO 691G	Bristol LH6L	Duple C41F	5/69	New
436	YBL 925H	Bristol LH6L	Duple C41F	5/70	New
437	YBL 926H	Bristol LH6L	Duple C41F	5/70	New
438	YBL 927H	Bristol LH6L	Duple C41F	7/70	New
439	YBL 928H	Bristol LH6L	Duple C41F	9/70	New

Two reminders of past South Midland glory.

Above – No.63 (NJO 217), an AEC 'Regal' of 1949, shown in its original livery of red, white and black, in the High Street, High Wycombe on the former United Counties Oxford – London route. The immaculate condition of this coach typifies the high standard of turnout of the fleet. Below – A varied selection of coaches were transferred or loaned from the Thames Valley fleet. Undoubtably the most classic vehicles to wear the maroon and cream livery were the Windover-bodied Bristol L6B's new to TV in 1950. No.545 (FMO 20) was used throughout the Summer of 1960, and is again in notably fine condition when seen at Victoria Coach Station.

Fleet List   From Charabanc to Luxury Coach

F.No.	Reg. No.	Chassis Make & Type	Bodybuilder	Layout	New	Acq.	Sold	Notes
	FC 3902	Dennis 2.5 ton	Dennis	Ch30	Apr-21	New	By 1931	
	FC 4010	Dennis 2.5 ton	Dennis	Ch30	May-21	New	By 1931	
	FC 4501	Dennis 2.5 ton	Dennis	Ch30	May-22	New	By 1931	
	LK 8069	Crossley	??	Ch16	??	c.1923	By 1931	
	FC 8130	Dennis 2.5 ton	??	Ch29D	Apr-25	New	By 1932	
	BL 1351	Hotchkiss 30/40hp	??	Ch14	May-14	by Jul-28	c.Oct-28	
	WL 2696	Lancia Pentaiota 35hp	??	Ch24D	Jun-27	New	c.May 1934	
	WL 4131	Lancia Pentaiota 35hp	Weymann	Ch26D	Feb-28	New	May-35	
14	WL 5055	Lancia Pentaiota 35hp	??	Ch28D	May-28	New	Jun-35	
15	WL 7221	Dennis GL	Arnold & Comben	Ch20D	May-29	New	Apr-32	
16	WL 7240	Dennis F	Arnold & Comben	Ch28D	Jun-29	New	May-37	
17	WL 7456	Dennis F	Arnold & Comben	Ch28D	Jun-29	New	May-37	
18	WL 7233	Gilford 166SD	Arnold & Comben	Ch26D	May-29	New	May-39	
19	WL 9058	Gilford 168OT	Arnold & Comben	Ch30F	Feb-30	New	Jun-45	
20	WL 9076	Gilford 168OT	Arnold & Comben	Ch30F	Mar-30	New	Feb-40	To WD
21	WL 9079	Gilford 168OT	Arnold & Comben	Ch28F	Mar-30	New	Jun-36	
22	WL 9081	Gilford 168OT	Arnold & Comben	Ch30F	Apr-30	New	Jun-39	
23	WL 9415	Gilford 168OT	Arnold & Comben	Ch30F	Apr-30	New	Mar-35	
24	WL 9810	Gilford 168OT	Arnold & Comben	Ch30F	May-30	New	Jan-35	
25	WL 9862	Gilford 168OT	Arnold & Comben	Ch30F	May-30	New	Oct-35	
26	WL 9942	Gilford 168OT	Arnold & Comben	Ch28F	Jun-30	New	May-39	
27	JO 200	Gilford 168OT	Arnold & Comben	Ch32F	Aug-30	New	Feb-35	
28	JO 1597	Leyland Tiger TS3	Scammell & Nephew	Ch28C	Mar-31	New	by Feb-51	
29	JO 1599	Leyland Tiger TS3	Scammell & Nephew	Ch28C	Mar-31	New	by Sep-50	
30	JO 1593	Leyland Tiger TS3	Scammell & Nephew	Ch28C	Apr-31	New	by Feb-52	
31	JO 1595	Leyland Tiger TS3	Scammell & Nephew	Ch28C	Apr-31	New	by Sep-50	
32	JO 4789	Leyland Tiger TS4	Harrington	Ch32R	Jun-32	New	by Sep-50	

F.No.	Reg. No.	Chassis Make & Type	Bodybuilder	Layout	New	Acq.	Sold	Notes
33	AFC 531	Leyland Tiger TS6	Harrington	C32F	May-34	New	c.Mar-1940	To WD
23?	HA 7493	Morris-Commercial Viceroy	??	C20F	Jul-31	1935?	c.1940	
34	BFC 675	Leyland Tiger TS7 oil	Harrington	C32F	Apr-35	New	Sep-50	
35	BWL 349	Leyland Tiger TS7 oil	Harrington	C32R	May-35	New	Jan-50	To N&D
36	CWL 951	Leyland Tiger TS7 oil	Harrington	C32F	Apr-36	New	Jan-50	To N&D
37	CWL 953	Leyland Tiger TS7 oil	Harrington	C32F	Apr-36	New	Jan-50	To N&D
24	FWL 795	Leyland Cub SKPZ2	Harrington	C26F	Mar-38	New	by Oct-47	
25	FWL 797	Leyland Cub SKPZ2	Harrington	C26F	Feb-38	New	by Oct-47	
26	HFC 548	Leyland Cheetah LZ2A	Burlingham	C32F	Mar-39	New	by Dec-47	
27	HFC 550	Leyland Cheetah LZ2A	Burlingham	C32F	Mar-39	New	by Oct-47	
23	JFC 12	Austin K3	Burlingham	C26F	Aug-39	New	May-48	
22	JFC 42	Austin K3	Harrington	C26F	Aug-39	New	May-48	
21	JFC 707	Austin K3	Harrington	C26F	1940	New	May-48	
38	LWL 995	Leyland Tiger PS1/1	ECOC (new 1936)	DP31R	Feb-47	New	Jan-50	To N&D
39	LWL 996	AEC Regal 0662	Duple	C33F	May-47	New	Jul-58	
40	LWL 997	AEC Regal 0662	Duple	C33F	May-47	New	Jul-58	
41	LWL 998	AEC Regal 0662	Duple	C33F	May-47	New	Oct-58	
42	LWL 999	AEC Regal 0662	Duple	C33F	May-47	New	Jul-58	
43	LJO 756	Bedford OB	Duple	C29F	Jul-47	New	Jan-50	To N&D
44	LJO 757	Bedford OB	Duple	C29F	Mar-48	New	Jan-50	To N&D
233	EM 2723	Albion PW65 (5LW)	Burlingham (new 1944)	UB34F	Jul-32	Jun-47	Jan-48	Ex R&W
251	EM 2743	Albion PW65 (5LW)	Burlingham (new 1944)	UB34F	Dec-32	Jun-47	Jan-48	Ex R&W
45	LJO 758	AEC Regal 0662	Duple	C33F	Aug-47	New	Oct-57	
46	LJO 759	AEC Regal 0662	Duple	C33F	Aug-47	New	Oct-58	
47	LJO 760	AEC Regal 0662	Duple	C33F	Aug-47	New	Oct-58	
48	LJO 761	AEC Regal 0662	Duple	C33F	Jan-48	New	Oct-57	
49	MWL 741	AEC Regal 0662	Duple	C33F	Jan-48	New	Oct-58	
50	MWL 742	AEC Regal 0662	Duple	C33F	Jan-48	New	Oct-58	
51	MWL 743	AEC Regal 0662	Duple	C33F	Jan-48	New	Aug-58	

F.No.	Reg. No.	Chassis Make & Type	Bodybuilder	Layout	New	Acq.	Sold	Notes
52	MWL 744	AEC Regal 0662	Duple	C33F	Jan-48	New	Oct-57	
53	MJO 278	AEC Regal 0662	Duple	C33F	Jan-48	New	Dec-58	
54	MJO 664	AEC Regal III 0682	Duple	C33F	Mar-48	New	Dec-58	
55	MJO 665	AEC Regal III 0682	Duple	C33F	Apr-48	New	Dec-58	
56	MJO 667	AEC Regal III 0682	Duple	C33F	Apr-48	New	Nov-59	
57	NFC 128	AEC Regal III 0682A	Duple	C33F	Sep-48	New	Nov-59	
58	NFC 129	AEC Regal III 0682A	Duple	C33F	May-49	New	Nov-59	
59	NFC 130	AEC Regal III 0682A	Duple	C33F	May-49	New	Nov-59	
60	NWL 877	AEC Regal III 0682A	Duple	C30F	Jun-49	New	Dec-58	
61	MWL 878	AEC Regal III 0682A	Duple	C30F	Jun-49	New	Jan-59	
62	MWL 879	AEC Regal III 0682A	Duple	C30F	Jun-49	New	Oct-57	
63	NJO 217	AEC Regal III 0682A	Duple	C30F	Jul-49	New	Jan-59	
64	NJO 218	AEC Regal III 0682A	Duple	C30F	Jul-49	New	Jan-59	
7	HAX 657	Bedford OB	Duple	C29F	Jun-49	Jun-49	Sep-49	Ex LM
8	HAX 828	Bedford OB	Duple	C29F	Jun-49	Sep-49	Sep-49	Ex LM
65	OFC 204	AEC Regal III 0682A	Duple	C30F	Mar-50	New	Jan-59	
66	OFC 205	AEC Regal III 0682A	Duple	C30F	Mar-50	New	Jan-59	
67	OFC 206	AEC Regal III 0682A	Duple	C30F	Mar-50	New	Jan-59	
68	EJB 649	AEC Regal III 0682A	Duple	C33F	Sep-48	Jan-50	Oct-59	Ex N&D
69	EJB 650	AEC Regal III 0682A	Duple	C33F	Sep-48	Jan-50	Jul-58	Ex N&D
70	ERX 937	AEC Regal III 0682A	Duple	C33F	Jul-49	Jan-50	Feb-60	Ex N&D
71	EBD 234	Bristol L6B	ECW	DP31R	Aug-48	May-52	Feb-53	Ex UC
72	EBD 235	Bristol L6B	ECW	DP31R	Sep-48	May-52	Feb-53	Ex UC
73	EBD 236	Bristol L6B	ECW	FC31F	May-50	May-52	Oct-61	Ex UC
74	EBD 237	Bristol L6B	ECW	FC31F	May-50	May-52	Nov-60	Ex UC
75	FRP 832	Bristol LL6B	ECW (8ft wide)	FC37F	Feb-51	May-52	Dec-62	Ex UC
76	FRP 833	Bristol LL6B	ECW (8ft wide)	FC37F	Feb-51	May-52	May-63	Ex UC
77	FRP 834	Bristol LL6B	ECW (8ft wide)	FC37F	Feb-51	May-52	Aug-63	Ex UC
78	FRP 836	Bristol LL6B	ECW (8ft wide)	FC37F	Feb-51	May-52	Mar-63	Ex UC
UC951	JWO 213	Leyland Royal Tiger PSU1/13	Lydney	C41F	Apr-52	May-52	Nov-52	Ex R&W

F.No.	Reg. No.	Chassis Make & Type	Bodybuilder	Layout	New	Acq.	Sold	Notes
UC2051	JWO 546	Leyland Royal Tiger PSU1/13	Lydney	C41F	Apr-52	May-52	Nov-52	Ex R&W
79	SFC 565	Bristol LS6G	ECW	C37F	Jun-52	New	Sep-65	
80	SFC 566	Bristol LS6G	ECW	C37F	Jun-52	New	Sep-65	
81	SFC 567	Bristol LS6G	ECW	C37F	Jun-52	New	Sep-65	
82	SFC 568	Bristol LS6G	ECW	C37F	Oct-52	New	Sep-65	
83	SFC 569	Bristol LS6G	ECW	C37F	Oct-52	New	Sep-65	
84	SFC 570	Bristol LS6G	ECW	C37F	Oct-52	New	Oct-61	
85	SFC 571	AEC Regal IV 9821E	ECW	C37F	Aug-52	New	Oct-67	
86	SFC 501	Guy Arab UF 6HLW	Lydney/BBW	C41C	Apr-53	New	Jul-60	To R&W
87	SFC 502	Guy Arab UF 6HLW	Lydney/BBW	C41C	May-53	New	Jul-60	To R&W
88	SFC 503	Guy Arab UF 6HLW	Lydney/BBW	C41C	Mar-53	New	Jul-60	To R&W
89	SFC 504	Guy Arab UF 6HLW	Lydney/BBW	C41C	Apr-53	New	Jul-60	To R&W
90	TWL 55	Bristol LS6B	ECW	C37F	Jun-53	New	Oct-65	To TV
91	TWL 56	Bristol LS6B	ECW	C37F	Jun-53	New	Nov-65	To TV
92	TWL 57	Bristol LS6B	ECW	C37F	Jun-53	New	Feb-66	To TV
93	TWL 58	Bristol LS6B	ECW	C37F	Jul-53	New	Feb-66	To TV
94	TWL 59	Bristol LS6B	ECW	C37F	Aug-53	New	Dec-66	To TV
95	TWL 60	Bristol LS6B	ECW	C37F	Oct-53	New	Apr-66	To TV
548	FMO 23	Bristol L6B	Windover	C33F	Mar-50	Jan-55	Oct-58	Ex TV
553	FMO 935	Bristol L6B	Windover	C33F	Jul-50	Jan-55	Oct-60	Ex TV
770	CAP 206	Bristol K5G	ECW/BH&D	OT56R	Aug-40	Jul-57	Jul-60	Ex TV
169	LWL 995	Leyland Tiger PS1/1	ECW (8ft wide)	FC34F	Feb-47	Jun-58	Oct-58	Ex N&D
800	ORX 631	Bristol MW6G	ECW	C34F	Mar-58	New	Dec-68	To TV
801	ORX 632	Bristol MW6G	ECW	C34F	Mar-58	New	Mar-69	To TV
802	ORX 633	Bristol MW6G	ECW	C34F	Apr-58	New	Mar-69	To TV
803	ORX 634	Bristol MW6G	ECW	C32F	Apr-58	New	Dec-68	To TV
689	HMO 835	Bristol LS6B	ECW	C39F	Oct-53	Jun-58	Nov-63	To TV
690	HMO 836	Bristol LS6B	ECW	C39F	Oct-53	Jun-58	Nov-63	To TV
692	HMO 838	Bristol LS6B	ECW	C39F	Feb-54	Jun-58	Dec-64	To TV

F.No.	Reg. No.	Chassis Make & Type	Bodybuilder	Layout	New	Acq.	Sold	Notes
693	HMO 839	Bristol LS6B	ECW	C39F	Feb-54	Jun-58	Feb-61	To TV
804	PRX 930	Bristol MW6G	ECW	C34F	Mar-59	New	Oct-69	To TV
805	PRX 931	Bristol MW6G	ECW	C34F	Apr-59	New	Oct-69	To TV
806	PRX 932	Bristol MW6G	ECW	C34F	Apr-59	New	Dec-69	To TV
807	PRX 933	Bristol MW6G	ECW	C34F	Mar-59	New	Aug-69	To TV
821	FRP 835	Bristol LL6B (8ft wide axles)	ECW (8ft wide)	FC37F	Feb-51	Jan-59	Oct-61	Ex UC
822	FRP 837	Bristol LL6B (8ft wide axles)	ECW (8ft wide)	FC37F	Feb-51	Jan-59	Mar-62	Ex UC
823	FRP 838	Bristol LL6B (8ft wide axles)	ECW (8ft wide)	FC37F	Mar-51	Jan-59	Jul-63	Ex UC
824	FRP 839	Bristol LL6B (8ft wide axles)	ECW (8ft wide)	FC37F	Feb-51	Jan-59	Mar-62	Ex UC
825	FRP 840	Bristol LL6B (8ft wide axles)	ECW (8ft wide)	FC37F	Mar-51	Jan-59	Jan-62	Ex UC
826	FRP 841	Bristol LL6B (8ft wide axles)	ECW (8ft wide)	FC37F	Feb-51	Jan-59	Oct-61	Ex UC
827	FRP 842	Bristol LL6B (8ft wide axles)	ECW (8ft wide)	FC37F	Feb-51	Jan-59	Mar-62	Ex UC
830	UJB 196	Bristol MW6G	ECW	C34F	Mar-60	New	Sep-70	To TV
831	UJB 197	Bristol MW6G	ECW	C34F	Mar-60	New	Jan-71	To CO
832	UJB 198	Bristol MW6G	ECW	C34F	Mar-60	New	Jan-71	To CO
552	FMO 934	Bristol L6B	Windover	C33F	Jun-50	Mar-60	Oct-60	Ex TV
833	UJB 199	Bristol MW6G	ECW	C34F	Apr-60	New	Jan-71	To CO
545	FMO 20	Bristol L6B	Windover	C33F	Jun-50	Jun-60	Oct-60	Ex TV
551	FMO 26	Bristol L6B	Windover	C33F	Jun-50	Jun-60	Nov-61	Ex TV
554	FMO 936	Bristol L6B	Windover	C33F	Jul-50	Jun-60	Oct-60	Ex TV
555	FMO 937	Bristol L6B	Windover	C33F	Jul-50	Jun-60	Oct-60	Ex TV
550	FMO 25	Bristol L6B	Windover	C33F	Jun-50	Jul-60	Oct-60	Ex TV
608	GBL 872	Bristol LWL6B	ECW	FC37F	Jul-51	Jul-60	Apr-64	Ex TV
609	GBL 873	Bristol LWL6B	ECW	FC37F	Aug-51	Jul-60	May-64	Ex TV
858	WRX 773	Bristol MW6G	ECW	C34F	May-61	New	Jan-71	To CO
859	WRX 774	Bristol MW6G	ECW	C34F	May-61	New	Jan-71	To CO
860	WRX 775	Bristol MW6G	ECW	C34F	Jun-61	New	Jan-71	To CO
861	WRX 776	Bedford SB8 (7ft 6ins wide)	Duple Super Vega	C37F	May-61	New	Feb-68	
673	HBL 75	Bristol LS6G	ECW	C39F	Jul-52	Dec-61	Oct-65	Ex TV
688	HMO 834	Bristol LS6B	ECW	C39F	Oct-53	Dec-61	Oct-64	Ex TV

F.No.	Reg. No.	Chassis Make & Type	Bodybuilder	Layout	New	Acq.	Sold	Notes
691	HMO 837	Bristol LS6B	ECW	C39F	Feb-54	Jan-62	Nov-63	Ex TV
610	GBL 874	Bristol LWL6B	ECW	FC37F	Aug-51	Mar-62	Apr-64	Ex TV
671	HBL 73	Bristol LS6G	ECW	C39F	Jul-52	Mar-62	Oct-67	Ex TV
862	516 ABL	Bedford SB8 (7ft 6ins wide)	Duple Super Vega	C37F	May-62	New	Apr-65	Ex TV
863	517 ABL	Bedford SB8 (8ft wide)	Duple Super Vega	C37F	May-62	New	Apr-65	Ex TV
864	518 ABL	Bedford SB8 (8ft wide)	Duple Super Vega	C37F	May-62	New	May-68	
865	519 ABL	Bedford SB8 (8ft wide)	Duple Super Vega	C37F	May-62	New	Jun-68	
867	521 ABL	Bristol REX6G (high floor)	ECW	C47F	Apr-63	New	Jan-71	To CO
C401	831 CRX	Bedford SB8	Duple Bella Vega	C37F	Feb-63	New	Oct-68	
C402	832 CRX	Bedford SB8	Duple Bella Vega	C37F	Apr-63	New	Oct-68	
C403	833 CRX	Bedford SB8	Duple Bella Vega	C37F	Apr-63	New	Oct-68	
674	HBL 76	Bristol LS6G	ECW	C39F	Sep-52	Jul-63	Nov-66	Ex TV
C404	834 CRX	Bristol RELH6G	ECW	C47F	Jan-64	New	Jan-71	To CO
C405	835 CRX	Bristol RELH6G	ECW	C47F	Jan-64	New	Jan-71	To CO
C407	837 CRX	Bedford SB13	Duple Super Vega	C37F	Jan-64	New	Sep-70	
C408	838 CRX	Bedford SB13	Duple Super Vega	C37F	Jan-64	New	Jul-70	To TV
C409	842 CRX	Bedford SB13	Duple Super Vega	C37F	Jan-64	New	Sep-70	
C410	EMO 551C	Bedford SB13	Harrington Crusader IV	C37F	Mar-65	New	Jan-71	To CO
C411	EMO 552C	Bedford SB13	Harrington Crusader IV	C37F	Mar-65	New	Jan-71	To CO
C412	EMO 553C	Bedford SB13	Harrington Crusader IV	C37F	Mar-65	New	Jan-71	To CO
672	HBL 74	Bristol LS6G	ECW	C39F	Jul-52	Apr-65	Aug-66	Ex TV
C413	GRX 413D	Bedford VAM14	Duple Bella Venture	C41F	Dec-65	New	Jan-71	To CO
C414	GRX 414D	Bedford VAM14	Duple Bella Venture	C41F	Dec-65	New	Jan-71	To CO
C415	GRX 415D	Bedford VAM14	Duple Bella Venture	C41F	Mar-66	New	Jan-71	To CO
C416	GRX 416D	Bedford VAM14	Duple Bella Venture	C41F	Mar-66	New	Jan-71	To CO
866	520 ABL	Bristol MW6G	ECW	C39F	Apr-62	May-66	Dec-66	Ex TV
675	HBL 77	Bristol LS6G	ECW	C39F	Sep-52	Dec-66	Aug-67	Ex TV
C421	LJB 421E	Bristol RELH6G	ECW	C47F	Apr-67	New	Jan-71	To CO
C422	LJB 422E	Bristol RELH6G	ECW	C47F	May-67	New	Jan-71	To CO

F.No.	Reg. No.	Chassis Make & Type	Bodybuilder	Layout	New	Acq.	Sold	Notes
C423	LJB 423E	Bristol RELH6G	ECW	C47F	May-67	New	Jan-71	To CO
C428	RJB 428F	Bristol LH6L	Duple Commander III	C41F	May-68	New	Jan-71	To CO
C429	RJB 429F	Bristol LH6L	Duple Commander III	C41F	May-68	New	Jan-71	To CO
C430	RJB 430F	Bristol LH6L	Duple Commander III	C41F	May-68	New	Jan-71	To CO
C431	RJB 431F	Bristol LH6L	Duple Commander III	C41F	May-68	New	Jan-71	To CO
C417	LJB 417E	Bedford VAM14	Duple Viceroy	C41F	Jan-67	May-68	Nov-70	Ex TV
C418	LJB 418E	Bedford VAM14	Duple Viceroy	C41F	Jan-67	May-68	Sep-69	Ex TV
C432	613 JPU	Bristol LS6G	ECW	C34F	Mar-57	Mar-69	Jan-71	Ex EN
C433	614 JPU	Bristol LS6G	ECW	C34F	Mar-57	Mar-69	Jan-71	Ex EN
C434	618 JPU	Bristol MW6G	ECW	C34F	Jan-58	Mar-69	Jan-71	Ex EN
432	UMO 688G	Bristol LH6L	Duple Commander IV	C41F	May-69	New	Jan-71	To CO
433	UMO 689G	Bristol LH6L	Duple Commander IV	C41F	May-69	New	Jan-71	To CO
434	UMO 690G	Bristol LH6L	Duple Commander IV	C41F	May-69	New	Jan-71	To CO
435	UMO 691G	Bristol LH6L	Duple Commander IV	C41F	May-69	New	Jan-71	To CO
436	YBL 925H	Bristol LH6L	Duple Commander IV	C41F	May-70	New	Jan-71	To CO
437	YBL 926H	Bristol LH6L	Duple Commander IV	C41F	May-70	New	Jan-71	To CO
438	YBL 927H	Bristol LH6L	Duple Commander IV	C41F	Jul-70	New	Jan-71	To CO
439	YBL 928H	Bristol LH6L	Duple Commander IV	C41F	Sep-70	New	Jan-71	To CO

Notes: A Dennis G-type chassis number 70388 was laid down for South Midland in January 1929, but is believed to have been superceded by the GL supplied.

A Leyland TS11 chassis with oil engine was ordered during 1940 but not delivered.

190

Notes:	To WD	Requistionned by War Dept.
	To N&D	Transferred to Newbury & District Motor Services Ltd.
	Ex N&D	Transferred from Newbury & District Motor Services Ltd.
	Ex R&W	On loan from Red & White & United Transport Services Ltd.
	Ex LM	On loan from Liberty Motors Ltd. (a R&W subsidary)
	Ex UC	Purchased from United Counties Omnibus Co. Ltd.
	To TV	Transferred to Thames Valley Traction Co. Ltd.
	Ex TV	Transferred from Thames Valley Traction Co. Ltd.
	Ex EN	Purchased from Eastern National Omnibus Co. Ltd.
	To CO	Taken over by City of Oxford Motor Services Ltd.

Standard Body Codes:

C	Before seating capacity indicates a coach body.
F	Before the above C indicates a fully-fronted body on a chassis type with front engine usually with half-cab body.
Ch	Before seating capacity indicates a charabanc body, i.e. with multiple doors and full-width seating.
B	Before seating capacity indicates a single-deck bus body fitted with bus-type seating.
DP	Before seating capacity indicates a single-deck bus body fitted with coach-type seating.
OT	Before seating capacity indicates an open-top double-deck bus.
Seats	These are indicated by the number within the code.
F	After seating capacity indicates a front entrance.
D	After seating capacity indicates a dual-entrance layout of front and rear doors.
R	After seating capacity indicates a rear entrance.

Example - FC31F indicates a fully-fronted coach with 31 seats and a front entrance.

191

South Midland coaches of the Thames Valley era. *Above- No.84 (SFC 570), a 1952 Bristol LS6G with Eastern Coach Works C37F body, seen in original cream and red livery at Victoria Coach Station. Below- Guy 'Arab' UF No.88 (SFC 503), also with a Gardner 6HLW engine, carried a Lydney Coach Works C41C body, being a vehicle originally ordered under Red & White control but not delivered until 1953. It wears the maroon and cream livery introduced in 1958, which made these heavyweight coaches look even more solid! The windscreen arrangement and high side windows were inspired by the body design used for the contemporary Leyland 'Royal Tiger' chassis and was particularly suited to express coach duties.*